Your Radiant Soul is an absolute treasure!

I came to this book with curiosity and an assumption that a journey into the world of "soul" and "energy" was somewhat beyond me. Yet, reading this book, my perspective, and even beliefs, have changed. Prune Harris, in this beautifully written book, delves deep into the power, the possibility, and the magic of this work. Above all, she makes it accessible, and it is a joyful read. I strongly recommend this book to anyone who is not only ready to make real, sustainable change in the way they see the world, but also ready to use energy and the soul's journey to transform their life. It's truly a wonder and a treasure!

~Lisa Bloom
Story Coach, Author, and podcast host of *Once Upon a Business*

Prune is a master educator who has been able to see energy since she was born. In this book, she welcomes us into her world, sharing information and practices using simple terms and everyday language that we can ingest in our own time to help us understand and activate the principles of the human energy system as the foundation of our health.

Throughout the chapters of this book, we learn that at a soul level, we are here to shine our light in everything we do and how we choose to be. However, we can get stuck in the endless doing of our busy lives, unable to fulfill our potential, and illness may even result. Through personal stories, case studies, insights, and accessible practices, Prune invites us to be curious about ourselves, to trust our choices, and actively and consciously engage with our lives. We can then step beyond our constricting patterns of limitation, feel joyful and empowered, and BE the medicine we need right now.

~Dr. Clare Willocks

Bridging the Health Care Gap/Nurture Your Energy

We all have a radiant soul, and through our actions and interactions (with other beings, our environment, and even ourselves), we all make constant contributions to our world through our unique energy signature. Prune Harris identifies three vibrational themes to this process: thinking, feeling, and doing. This is a timely, transformative, and empowering book by a master teacher, which many have been waiting for! Gift yourself this book and use it daily to unlock your full energetic and creative potential!

~Imelda Almqvist

International teacher of *Sacred Art and Seiðr*, author of *Medicine of the Imagination* and *North Sea Water In My Veins*

Your Radiant Soul is a treasure trove filled with vital, life changing information. It is a book I wish I could have read early in life, and one that I will readily recommend to my clients, students, and friends. Prune Harris has a great gift, not only in being able to see energy and clearly explain the intricacies of the human energy system, but even more importantly, how to use that information to transform our lives.

Her deep knowledge, broad experience, and uplifting passion are palpable on each page, as she shares her spiritual insights, motivating examples, and empowering practices. Something that is rarely included elsewhere is her recognition of different learning styles. At the end of each chapter, the reader is invited to experience the information just covered through thinking, feeling, and/or doing practices, which greatly facilitate its integration and implementation. While there are many books on energy and healing, in my experience, Prune Harris' Your Radiant Soul excels in its lucidity, usefulness, and power to inspire.

~Stephanie Austin, M.A.
Astrological counselor, teacher, and writer

I profoundly welcome Prune's book. Her informative and encouraging approach provides essential waymarkers, navigational aids, key understandings and practices important for those who seek to engage in a journey of self care beyond the knowledge boundaries of conventional perspectives on health. It equally will provide new insights and strengthen understandings for those who are already on such a journey.

Prune's understandings are new-old; I say that because I believe they sit comfortably alongside understandings voiced by various Mi'kmaw Indigenous Elders and educators in Unama'ki/Cape Breton with whom I've been blessed to laugh-learn-work with over two decades. Prune's approach also fits comfortably within the Mi'kmaw principle of 'Etuaptmumk' or 'Two-Eyed Seeing,' encouraging us to learn to see with both the strengths of conventional knowledge and ways of knowing and with the strengths of the wholistically richer Indigenous knowledge and ways of knowing. Prune's book is a superb contribution that will help enable enriched seeing, learning, and being for those who choose the journey of agency towards self-care and well-being within relationships – reciprocity – respect – responsibility in a vibrant and nurturing Cosmos. From my own life experience, I can testify that Prune's practices, guidance, and teachings have stretched me in the most wholesome of ways. And such is my wish for all who are interested.

~Cheryl M. Bartlett, CM, PhD
Professor Emerita of Biology and Integrative Science,
Cape Breton University

Having had the privilege of experiencing Prune teach in the classroom, I experienced once again her joyful enthusiasm in this remarkable summary of her understanding of the integrated, energetic nature of our bodies and our interconnectedness with all things. Prune is a medical intuitive who perceives illness as it shows up in our energy systems through shifts in colour and changes in flow. Revealing a breadth of learning about diverse theories of health, Prune maps her own felt experience onto the wisdom of a wide range of holistic health systems to describe the energetic anatomy of the body, throughout offering practical practices for enabling energetic flexibility, practices she has shared with many students in her teaching programmes. Her book concludes with a summary of the overarching determinants of

holistic health or resilience; the cultivation of a sense of belonging, kindness to self and all creation, and allowing one's wild wisdom, the intuition, to have the freedom to shape our destiny. This is a book which offers hope that healing and wholeness is always within our grasp and offers us some strategies about how we might begin to claim these gifts for ourselves and for those around us.

~Dr. Clare Stephenson

Author of *The Acupuncturist's Guide to Conventional Medicine*

Would you like to have a clear understanding of how your body produces sickness and health and why? Prune's vast knowledge and years of experience of seeing energy gives us a unique understanding of exactly this—you will find information in this book that you have never come across anywhere else!

Whether you're a beginner or an advanced practitioner, this book is full of practical everyday tips which can improve your health, happiness, and well-being, and give you clarity around what you need to work on and why.

Prune's clear vision and extensive experience is a blessing for those of us who want to know how to thrive. Keep this book on your shelf somewhere close at hand to refer to often. Then as you carry out the fun, effective, and powerful practices and techniques to create the life that you want and deserve to have, you'll just love this book more and more.

Thank you, Prune, for sharing your gifts and wisdom so generously with us all!

~Rachel Goodwin

Author of (Ascended Master) *Sarah's Little Book of Healing*

I became friends with Prune over a two-year course in Norse Shamanism that became four because of Covid. In that kind of environment, there are many unexpected learnings, and some of the deepest came from working with Prune. It is rare to meet someone who can navigate between the sacred and profane so naturally and easily, to be able to plunge deeply into shadow work, and then to be able to share a joke about it afterwards. I found her contributions in the group to be casually wise and I have never seen her lose her centre. I aspire to reach that level of grounded spirituality.

If I were to choose a teacher, it would be Prune, and I think in this book you'll find many reasons to agree with me. We urgently need to reconnect to the energy that surrounds us, and the place to start has to be by reconnecting with our own. Allow this book to be your guide.

~Trevor Silvester

Author and co-founder of *The Quest Institute*

This book makes my heart sing! Through it, Prune takes us on an empowering and transformative journey, sharing understandings and practices to support us to connect and come home to our personal guiding light.

Your Radiant Soul is a remembering of our unique strengths, gifts, and blessings both as an individual, and as a vital thread in the web of life.

By deepening our understanding of energy, Prune offers us the ability to create empowered choices that are in alignment with our soul essence. I have loved reading her wealth of wisdom through her case studies and her personal journey, and I am overjoyed knowing that this book will touch many people and create beautiful ripples of transformation into the collective.

Thank you, Prune.

~Sjoukje Gummels
Shamanic Practitioner

Prune writes about the human energy system from a place of such abundant passion, generosity of spirit, and compassion that you can never quite see or experience the world in the same way after having seen it through her eyes. It is a luminous book that reorients your world and remains a compass to navigate the human condition. Prune invites you to embody your Radiant Soul and make it visible in the world so that you can truly live the life that you came to experience and wholeheartedly belong to the world.

The book is a personal invitation to go on a journey of self-actualisation through the energetic landscape, embracing the mundane as well as the sacred, continually being inspired and empowered through the wisdom and exploration of the practices and techniques to evolve your energy system and expand your consciousness.

At the heart of this book is Prune's Wild Wisdom of sharing her gifts with humility for the evolution of human consciousness, and more than the human world, in service to life and beauty.

~Jyotish Patel

Facilitator of Transformation, Regenerative healthcare practitioner

From a gifted energy healer and a passionate teacher, Your Radiant Soul is an invitation to realise our full potential. This unique and practical guide shows us step by step how to move beyond the limits of the known and into an extraordinary new life, a new way of thinking, doing, and feeling. In a clear and straightforward style, Prune has woven into a single volume the ancient lessons of energy and how it works for each one of us, as well as the paradigm-altering discoveries of quantum science and how they all come together. In her 20+ years of clinical practice, Prune has bridged the knowledge of the past into the practice of the present. Prune shows us that we are so much more than just our linear minds. She starts where we are with very clear examples, definitions, and explanations on how she has experienced and seen energy. From there, she gives each one of us the opportunity to embrace this newfound wisdom into our own *lives through three practices at the end of each chapter. As you unfold into your understanding of how your energy system works, new ideas and possibilities jump forward and new ways of experiencing our world are at hand. This is a life changing, not to be missed read!*

~Valarie Budayr
Founder of Mongata Healing Center

Our Radiant Soul!!

After many years in private clinical practice, teaching in an academic setting, uploading multitudes of energy exercises to YouTube, then developing an online platform of life and soul enhancing classes, at last Prune Harris has gone the next step and written this profound book to further share her journey with a wider audience and capture the essence of her life's mission. That mission is not an easy one to encapsulate. Prune sees the beauty of each soul and imagines it at its highest potential, and I therefore don't believe she can rest until every human can also see the beauty and perfection in their energy anatomy, and be driven to allow it to shine.

This is full circle to Prune's original 'Imaginal Health' imagining, of how the world could be if only we could see how our beautiful energy is intertwined with the Cosmos/Universe/Web of Life. If we could see how luminescent and resilient we could be if we were 'in balance' with what matters (our unique relationship with Earth), then perhaps our behavior would improve.

This is a beautiful inspiring story of who we are, in reality and in potential, according to the revelations of the energies that Prune envisions. Don't read this book unless you want your life to be changed, as it is insightful and action-provoking.

Thank you Prune for the invitation to explore and be curious with our best selves and for insisting upon it!!

~Dr. Victoria Farthing DVM

YOUR
RADIANT
SOUL

YOUR
RADIANT
SOUL

Understand Your Energy to Transform Your World

Prune Harris

 Publish Your Purpose

For permission requests, write to the publisher, addressed "Attention: Permissions Coordinator," at the address below.

Publish Your Purpose
141 Weston Street, #155
Hartford, CT, 06141

 **Publish** Your Purpose

The opinions expressed by the Author are not necessarily those held by Publish Your Purpose.

Ordering Information: Quantity sales and special discounts are available on quantity purchases by corporations, associations, and others. For details, contact the publisher at hello@publishyourpurpose.com.

Edited by: Nancy Graham-Tillman, Chloe Siennah
Cover design by: Julia Kuris
Typeset by: Medlar Publishing Solutions Pvt Ltd., India
Illustrations by: Sandra Bernier, Alysha Takoushian

Printed in the United States of America.

ISBN: 979-8-88797-032-5 (hardcover)
ISBN: 979-8-88797-031-8 (paperback)
ISBN: 979-8-88797-033-2 (ebook)

Library of Congress Control Number: 2023903365

First edition, April 2023.

The information contained within this book is strictly for informational purposes. The material may include information, products, or services by third parties. As such, the Author and Publisher do not assume responsibility or liability for any third-party material or opinions. The publisher is not responsible for websites (or their content) that are not owned by the publisher. Readers are advised to do their own due diligence when it comes to making decisions.

Publish Your Purpose is a hybrid publisher of non-fiction books. Our mission is to elevate the voices often excluded from traditional publishing. We intentionally seek out authors and storytellers with diverse backgrounds, life experiences, and unique perspectives to publish books that will make an impact in the world. Do you have a book idea you would like us to consider publishing? Please visit PublishYourPurpose.com for more information.

DISCLAIMER

1. The names and identifying details of certain individuals have been changed to protect their privacy.

2. The information in this book is true and complete to the best of the author's knowledge. Any advice or recommendations are made without guarantee on the part of the author or publisher. The author and publisher disclaim any liability in connection with the use of this information.

3. The information provided within this book is for general informational and educational purposes only. The author makes no representations or warranties, express or implied, about the completeness, accuracy, reliability, suitability, or availability with respect to the information, products, services, or related graphics contained in this book for any purpose. Any use of this information is at your own risk.

DEDICATION

This book is dedicated to Hope and Love
and all who empower them.

And to my dad, Charlie Harris,
who inspired hope and embodied love
every day of his life.

CHERISHING LIFE

A Foreword by Caitlín Matthews
to *Your Radiant Soul* by Prune Harris

As a young child, I was always wishing that someone had written a handbook to humans so that I could learn how living worked, since so much of it went unexplained or unnoticed by the adults around me. I knew that there must be something I was not being told, because I could experience a much bigger life than the little lives lived out around me; this power seemed to bridge the two—the lesser and greater life— but no one ever spoke to me about it. I was given no vocabulary to discuss this extraordinary power and so, in my ignorance, I sang to this power all the time in order to remain connected with a larger supporting knowledge. It has taught me well over 70 years.

It is still the case today that one of the most neglected areas of our education is a basic understanding of how the energy of our life force works. Not being able to understand why things move us, and not being able to rebalance ourselves when we become out of kilter, makes us haphazard humans who are always swimming without direction through an unfathomable mystery. It is an exhausting way to live. The muddles of mind, heart, and body will always remain unresolved until we have discovered how the soul coordinates, heals, and harmonises.

Fortunately, in *Your Radiant Soul*, Prune Harris reveals how our life energy is wired so that everyone can have a practical understanding of how we can live more harmoniously. Energetic health lies within our power without our needing to learn esoteric skills. When we understand that our body and soul are connected to a much bigger energy field, we can learn how to repattern, refresh, and coordinate our whole system.

Dissolving fear, clearing away old assumptions, we can discern the actual patterning of our energetic vigour as a river that has always threaded us, body and soul—suddenly the map of our whole being is alight with understanding, as we find its elements, meridians, and pathways. This is the basis of a template of health that will never desert us. Through it, we learn that it is not the shielding of protection from the outside world that we need, but rather a connection to the greater energy field in which every life is living. As Prune reminds us, this radical belonging is a birthright, not an attainment for specially gifted people.

The basic kindness that loves ourselves as well as others, the acknowledgement of who we each are amid many, the trust that we can bring our own energetic networks into better calibration, all enables us to comprehend the essential exchange by which life is transmitted. For life energy cannot be hoarded: it is given and received everyday, like the breath in our lungs that breathes in and out of us. By cherishing the energy of life, we both serve it and are served by it—which, in every tradition, is reckoned to be a life well lived.

By Caitlín Matthews
Author of *Singing the Soul Back Home*
and *Psychic Protection Handbook*

ACKNOWLEDGEMENTS

Wow, what a journey it has been to birth this book. It is with great joy in my heart that I write these words of gratitude.

A happy and heartfelt THANK YOU to all the special people in my life who provide continual support and guidance to me as I navigate my big life, in all of its messy, wonderful, amazing, odd, joyful gifts and challenges. I would not be able to create my writings and teachings without you. This includes everyone in the team of brilliant people who form Prune Harris Ltd., each of whom have heard their soul calling to be an active part of creating a vision, a new story, and a new world.

A special thanks to Nat Hunter for your support and coaching when I was grappling with the many threads in my world and wondering just how to put them all together in a coherent book, and to Alison Moncrieff for holding the heart of this book and working so tirelessly to find its perfect pathway. Thanks to Jyotish Patel for walking this path with me with such wisdom and friendship. Thanks to Naomi Stewart for late night calls when I needed to bounce ideas around and to Emma Wagstaff for your tireless proofreading. Thanks to Sara and Brad Weyland and Jen Archibald for your encouragement and your requests for me to write a book in the first place!

A loud shout out to the two women who created all of the Energy Anatomy illustrations in this book and my work. Sandra Bernier and Alysha Takoushian, how you took my descriptions of what I see and turned them into beautiful visuals is awesome! Thank you.

I am very much in love with my publishers, Bailly Morse and Jenn Grace from Publish Your Purpose. Thank you for your guidance and for making the whole process of publishing this book easy and fun. Thank you to Nancy Graham-Tillman for your brilliant editing as well, each edit made my cells smile just a little bit deeper!

With happy humility and a touch of wonder, I honour and acknowledge my human teachers and their wisdom lineages, Nancy Finch (Mikao Usui Reiki), Katherine Bird (John Thie and Touch for Health), Dr. Cheryl Bartlett, Mi'kmaq First Nation Elders Albert and Murdena Marshall, Nancy Sherwood (Celtic and First Nations Shamanism), Caitlin Matthews (Celtic Shamanism and the Western Mystery Traditions), Donna Eden and David Feinstein (Energy Medicine and Energy Psychology), and Imelda Almqvist (Shamanic Healing and Seiðr\Old Norse Traditions). Each of your wisdoms have lit up my world and guided me deeper towards my own wild wisdom, for which I am forever grateful. This is also true of each of my clients and students throughout the years. I wish as well to give deepest gratitude and honour to my Spirit Teachers, Channelled Guides and the immense mystery teachings of the natural world.

My life is lived through my heart and soul, and here I give the deepest gratitude to my family, who guard them and cherish them so that even when I'm out in the further edges of the Cosmos, or fixated on the details of copy editing or class design, I am safe, understood, and beloved. It is your care and love that is my real superpower, and I recognise it, every minute of every day. So thank you, Collin, Rowan, and Ellarose. And thank you to my sister Jo for your courage, and for showing me how to always honour the joy of life (and always being happy to listen to me talk about my work, and think about my work, and dream about my work, and . . . You get the idea.) To all of my family and friends: I love each of you for your fierce hearts, your joy, and your courage to live fully. You inspire me every day.

Finally, and always, I honour and give gratitude to the ancestors of all times and realms, who guide me forward step by step, breath by breath. Together, may all of us co-create a world that will delight our descendants.

With love and in deepest thanks,

Prune

Illustration credits:

Sandra Bernier
https://sandrabernier.ca/
Alysha Takoushian
https://www.linkedin.com/in/alysha-takoushian-a38928178/

CONTENTS

INTRODUCTION

The ideals which have lighted my way, and time after time have given me new courage to face life cheerfully, have been Kindness, Beauty, and Truth.

~Albert Einstein
(1879–1955)

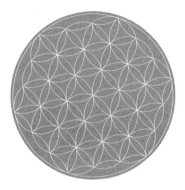

I am so delighted that you are here. Thank you. Through these pages we are going to go on a journey together, and my primary objective on this adventure is to remind you that you are powerful, you are wise, and you are packed with vast potential that can help transform not only *your* life, but life for all of us. You are an essential part of this great fabric of life, and if you are already here reading this, then it is because on one level you already know this, and on another you feel you have not quite stepped into it fully yet. But you can, and you will. My hope is that this book will provide some essential waymarkers and navigational aids for how to bring your vast and magnificent potential into your world every day.

I have been able to see energy since I was born – the energy systems of humans, animals, the natural world – and this means I am also able to see the energy of beings that exist without matter. My childhood was filled with seeing people other people could not see, whether they were those who had died and were now in the spirit world, or energies in nature or buildings. For me, this is all natural. As I grew up, I got glimpses of understanding that perhaps not everyone saw the world as I did, but it was not until my mid-30s that I began to understand my definition of "normal" was quite different from most everybody else's!

When I look at a person I can see them just as you do: the colour of their eyes, the tone of their skin, the clothes they are wearing, how tall they are, and what approximate age they are. Just like you I can perceive their emotional state whether they are happy, stressed, or angry, but I can also see the way their *energy* moves through, from, and around their body. In addition, I can see the energy centres in the human energy system and the places where these energy systems begin to interact with other energy systems, such as another person, an animal, or a tree. Looking at anyone, it is apparent to me where there is flow and balance in their physical and emotional health and where that flow and balance is compromised, depleted, or congested. Every emotion has a specific energy; every thought has a specific energy. If you are feeling joyous, your energy fields look very different than when you are feeling sad. This means I can see the energy of trauma and the energy of love, the energy of deceit and the energy of trust, the energy of despair and the energy of courage. I can see the energy at the very core of the human energy system, the deepest and most essential part of joy energy – one that you might call the soul. This is my normal.

Having spent 45 years observing the human energy system, 20 of those working with clients in clinical practice, as well as teaching thousands of students how to understand and balance their energy, I have no doubt that the human energy system is the foundation of our health. Understanding how to support our energy means being able to support our physical health, mental health, and vitality, because everything we are on a physical and emotional level, we are on an energetic level first.

When we understand how to support our energy fields, we become immensely powerful in our own lives. On a personal level, we no longer have to play out the old patterns of dysfunction or pain, and on a collective level, we realise that we are co-creators of the world in which we all live. When we are able to meet this awareness, we take our role in actively co-creating the world we want to live in, not the world we feel others are creating for us.

One of the fundamental truths that evolves from understanding our energy is that in every moment, every day, we have choice. Maybe you don't believe that yet. That's OK. You will, because it is a simple truth that is held in every part of your energy. In your exquisite flow and cohesion, your energy fields are fields of consciousness, and when you can understand how to nurture and balance them, you can enable transformation in your life and the lives of those around you.

It is quite a trip. Let's go!

Firstly, we are going to explore a bit more about your energy anatomy and how your energy systems connect to each other and to you. Then we will journey together through the energy of emotions and how you can bring balance, fullness, and healing to any part of your life you choose to focus on. Each chapter offers practices and techniques for you to explore.

Be aware that in any of the practices and techniques in this book, each section will activate different pathways of healing. Some you will immediately resonate with and love, others may be slow growers or not at all right for you. You are the only person who is going to be able to figure out which of these practices are the right ones for you. Get curious, get playful, and always assess how you feel before you do the practices and afterwards, or you will not have any way to begin to know which ones are the special keys to unlocking the health in your own amazing and unique energy system.

I have divided each of the practice sections into three categories: thinking, feeling, and doing. All of them activate and work on your energy fields, but they work in slightly different ways that will resonate with you uniquely. You may find you really connect to the "thinking" category or the "doing" category in each chapter, or you may find that sometimes you resonate with one category in one chapter but love a different category in another. Perhaps in the aura section you will love the practice in the "doing" category, while in the kindness practices you will love the "feeling" or "thinking" category. There is no right or wrong, and there is only one person who can truly understand your energy and how to best support it: YOU. Keep broad, remain expansive, and get curious. I have created videos of many of the practices I've put into this book so I can personally guide you as we do them together. You can find these videos and other supporting material at www.pruneharris.com/radiant-soul.

Each small task of everyday life

is part of the total harmony

of the universe.

~Therese of Lisieux

(1873–1897)

WE WOULD LOVE TO SUPPORT YOUR RADIANT SOUL JOURNEY

Get the most out of this book with;

- Video Guides – Let Prune guide you through the practices in this book.

- 3 Months Free Membership – Join our online community at The Gathering Ground where you can share, connect, and be inspired.

- Do you want to know your soul colour? – As a gift, we would like to give you Prune's book '*What is the colour of your soul?*'

Visit www.pruneharris.com/radiant-soul or scan the QR code

EVERYTHING
IS ENERGY

No problem can be solved from the same consciousness that created it. We must learn to see the world anew.

~Albert Einstein

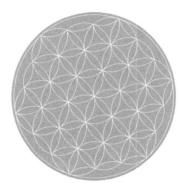

So, perhaps you have read the introduction and are thinking, "Wow, it's so cool that Prune can see energy." It *is* amazing, and I feel grateful every day for being able to have some things mapped out so simply for me, for when you see energy fields, the navigational aids for life are much more apparent! But I want to tell you a bit more about me and why I believe I can see energy.

I am one of twins and my twin died late in gestation. When I was born, I was premature, tiny, black, and wrinkled, hence the name Prune, and in some ways I was a real fighter; I was determined to live, not just for myself, but for my sister who was unable to live. On a deep level, before she died, we had contracted that one of us would live and that it would be me. For decades, I carried the responsibility of this contract with a sense of grief, loss, and deep longing for another plane of being. Only recently have I begun to realise my life for the immense and joyous gift that it was and still is.

I clearly remember coming into this world and being received by warm hands. The feeling of being touched on my skin was like thousands of warm electrical jolts, and my body responded with its own electrical sparks flying across my entire skin (which is deeply electrical in every person). At first, all I could see was energy, continually shape-shifting as people moved, talked, thought, and existed around me. Interestingly, I don't really remember sounds from those first few days. The energy of touch and the energy of life were my sensory understandings. And the nourishment of milk. As I drew milk into my throat for the first time and it moved through the centre of my body, the explosive energy of that sustenance, like shock, spread its incredible living energy through me. My physicality became more alive, more solid, and more corporeal as it coursed through me. Writing this now, I remember my mum telling me she had to physically lock the nurses out of the room each time she nursed me. I was born in the early '70s when the milk formula companies had done an excellent job of convincing the mainstream medical system to believe that their powdered, artificial product was far superior to breastmilk. It makes me admire the fierce protection of my mother's love, knowing she listened to her deep intuitive wisdom and locked that door!

Over those first few days, shapes became more solid, and I began seeing matter as well as energy. And I still had a strong energetic link with my twin, a link that has remained all my life.

As she moved in the otherworld, I was always connected to her, and I deeply believe that is why I was able to retain this ability to see energy.

Growing up, seeing energy was my norm. I didn't know any different. In buildings, I was scared a lot of the time. I could see people other people didn't seem to see, and I could see the places where otherworldly realms intersected with the human realm. Around every corner, there were translucent energies moving along and through the corridors of our house. Though I thought all of this was normal, it was still scary. I grew up in a house with several big dogs, and they would accompany me like a pack as I moved around the house. I developed the strategy of looking only at the dogs as I walked through the house and agreed with myself that if they weren't scared, then I didn't need to be either. But it didn't always work, and I would hold my breath from room to room, glad of bumping into a brother or sister to be with.

On my eighth birthday, I was given a dog of my own, a black-and-white spaniel I called Chianti. She was my shield and my courage and, unless I was at school or on a horse, we were inseparable. I can still feel how her energy wrapped itself around me whenever I was scared, and when I was awake in the night, she would be there, holding me safe and anchored to this world. So many children alive right now are experiencing the overwhelm of this kind of energetic sensitivity, and it is part of my work to bring increasingly more understanding to help support these children and, indeed, the many millions of sensitive adults who are still marginalised by societal norms.

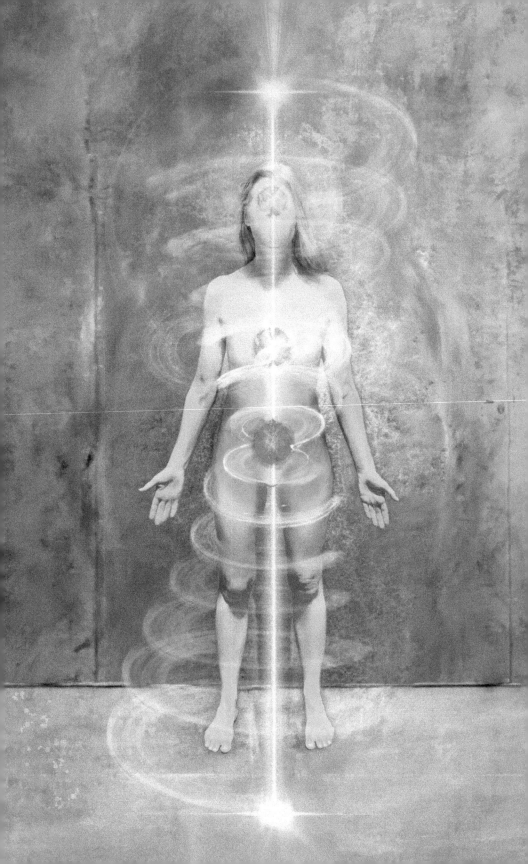

I spent a lot of time in nature. We had a smallholding with a few cows, goats, geese, chickens, and horses. I spent hours each day on horseback observing how the energies of human, animal, and nature continuously wove in and out of each other. This time spent with the natural world (including animals) is what I believe ensured that my understanding and perception of energy continued long after the ability ceases to be nurtured in other children.

My understanding of energy and the land trained me to speak the language of energy. And, hugely in my life, my horses provided me with quite literally my vehicle through this dynamic and vast world. They were, and remain, my greatest teachers.

People were a vibrant swirl of colours and noise. I grew up in a deeply loving and accepting family, learning the values of honesty, kindness, community living, and treating other people as you would like to be treated yourself. With two parents, six kids, and often many other people in the house for varying periods of time, there was always laughter, noise, and interaction. Time in nature and with my horses was my own time of deep communion when I had hours every day to be an apprentice to the energy of the world.

Your energy system is dynamic, interactive and interconnective. This image shows your energetic core, in its essential and awesome magnificence.

And yet with the energetic link to my twin a constant, there was always the deep, deep striving drive to be better, to do more, to be enough for not just one life, but two. Grief, loss, and uncertainty were masked by external success as I strove for perfection at school and in competitive sports. When another loss of a sibling occurred when I was 11, my system gradually moved towards overload. There is only so much imbalance that one human energy system can take, especially a super-sensitive one!

At age 16, my body went into a huge collapse, showing up as chronic fatigue syndrome (CFS) and putting me in bed for two years. Energetically, all cohesion was lost, and physically and emotionally, it felt like that too. I had pain in every muscle in my body, and my heart lost all its rhythm, sometimes crashing around and other times getting so quiet and infrequent that I wondered if it would stop completely. In those first few months, as my energy systems and health were giving up, I would regularly pass out mid-sentence, mid-meal, even mid-shop; one day my mum looked back to see me lying unconscious in an open freezer in a supermarket after I had been reaching for some frozen food!

My body was simply saying, "No more." I didn't have enough energy to get out of bed, digest any food, or even read more than a few sentences. In those two years I spent in bed, I travelled into the depth of my being and was initiated into the places beyond thought or understanding. In other (not so poetic) words, I crashed and burned, big time! It felt like I ceased to exist in every form of identity by which I had previously been created. I went from being a bright, energetic, fun, and lively young woman to not even being able to crawl out of bed.

Right now, when I think of it, I want to wrap my arms around that young woman and say, "It's OK, you will get through it," but if anyone had said that to me when I was experiencing it, I wouldn't have believed them. I *couldn't* have believed them. It felt like every ounce of my life force had left me. And what was I left with? Emptiness, pain, and a void so huge that I had no choice but to be in it, in all its darkness.

About 15 months into being in bed and in that darkness, I finally gave up trying. I found a place inside to rest, a place to feel all the pain I had been avoiding, a place to be, a place of accepting that I just didn't have any answers or even any clue as to what the questions were! None of my understanding of energy could help me figure out what was going on, nor could anyone else. Once the doctors had diagnosed me with CFS, people simply accepted that I would be like this for many years, maybe most of my life, or they thought I was making it up, it was "all in my head," and I should just go on a long bike ride and feel better.

And all the time there were two energies I could always see. The first was a vast ball of energy that was always present in a corner of my room. It spun like a portal, radiating energy out into the room. It was a constant; for over a year, it never changed and never moved from that one place. It simply spun, slowly radiating its soft yellow light. At times, I would talk to it, but mostly I just understood it was supportive and was there, simply being.

The second energy I could always see was the tiny, tiny flicker of my life force in my cells. There was no longer the huge, vibrant light in my body radiating out to others, trying to be enough, trying to bring balance and healing to their wounds and pains. Now there was just a tiny flicker of energy.

During this time, when I looked at my body, I could no longer see my skin or my tissue, for without the strength of my life force to emanate that through my physical body, I was left to navigate the energy fields alone. During the depths of that time, the only parts of my body that I could see were my bones (for they hold core energy that radiates even during extreme illness). The rest of my body was simply a greyish translucency, much like if you were to look at an X-ray.

Looking in the mirror was even more trippy, because I would see myself in the pyjamas I was wearing, all shape-shifty and X-ray translucent, but it would rarely be my face that looked back at me. Other faces sat on my bones, sometimes for seconds, sometimes for minutes. I would stare at those faces as they came in and left. It wasn't scary, or rather it wasn't any scarier than my usual odd experiences of seeing energy and forms. I had an awareness that all these faces belonged to people who were no longer alive and, somehow, in my place of near invisibility, I was seeing them through my own eyes.

They didn't feel supportive or threatening; they were simply part of a vast collective energy field I also belonged to.

Now I understand that these were the faces of my ancestors, showing through the ancestral energy field that is a constant in every person. Most were simply existing within that energy field, and I was looking through my own personage and into that family tree. Beautiful now when I think of it, but as a very ill 17 year old, I was simply faced with another question as to what on earth was happening in my life.

At some point during that phase, I noticed that when I read poetry, the flicker of energy in my body grew, just for a few minutes, and then faded. When Mum bought kittens to keep me company and they snuggled up with me, that flicker grew just a little bit. In my foggy brain, I wondered what else might enhance that life force, so I experimented with my diet. When I went on a strict elimination diet, my life force got stronger. I sat in the stables with my horse for the first time in over a year, and my life force became stronger even as I cried out in pain. The clearing had begun, and whatever imbalances had created my illness were beginning to move. In every part of me, I could see my energy begin to flicker back into being. The void I had lived in for 18 months was regenerating, and I knew I was fundamentally different in this rebirthing. I began placing my hands and arms on various parts of my body to help that life force spread and connect. I realised that if I breathed energy into my heart area, my heart would settle more; the erratic nature of its beating would quieten. If I curled up into a ball with my arms hugging my outer ribs, I could see my energy move through my skin. Little by little, tiny act by tiny act, I watched some colours return to my chakras as little sparks of light and colour flickering brighter. My skin became more visible; I could see my fingers and could see my own face in the mirror more frequently. I began to look solid again! Organs began to buzz and hum in their own special vibration and song. I was coming back.

It was another year of supporting myself and being supported with love, diet, and varying energy healing therapies before I could trust that I was going to recover fully. Towards the end of this three-year process, when I was out with friends – which in itself was a joyous miracle – I laughed at something that was happening and an explosion of healing surged throughout my entire body and energy systems. A roaring of colour and noise came from inside me, bursting from my core through everything I was. I almost couldn't breathe with the intensity of it, but at that point, CFS left me and my own energy reclaimed its vitality, balance, flow, and force. I have never looked back.

That is not to say that I have never experienced illness since that point, but with anything else that has come forward in my life, I knew I could understand and balance it within my system. I have healed from epilepsy, extreme heart problems, and breast cancer in this way because, perhaps not surprisingly, being super sensitive means my body responds to energy on every level, from the personal to the collective. It has been,

From deep in your energetic core, your assemblage point guides you forward, helping you align to your soul path every second of your life.

and continues to be, a life journey to ensure that the antennae connecting me so strongly to the psychic world don't negatively impact my physical body. Illness and disease point me towards places of imbalance within me, and I can then turn my focus to them and bring in the balance needed for real and lasting healing. From my 20s, I trained with healers throughout the world in many different disciplines to give myself the language and breadth of experience that increasingly bring these understandings into the everyday for thousands of clients and students.

And it feels more important than ever that everyone understands energy. Because you, too, are born with the ability to navigate the world of energy. In fact, that is exactly how you navigated life in the beginning, just like every other baby in the animal world. Throughout your life, your energy fields are the first places you determine safety or threat, which means that when you were born, you were able to perceive energy. This natural way of being likely stayed with you for the first several years of your life.

Have you been around newborn babies and watched what they watch? They are watching what perhaps you can no longer see, but they are seeing it. I love watching babies looking at the world. Sometimes their eyes are locked on your eyes, absorbing all kinds of information and energetic exchange, and oftentimes they are watching about one metre above your head. This is an exquisite part of your energy fields where your own energy meets and interacts with the energy of whatever is surrounding you. This energetic interface is a powerful and magical place packed with potential, consciousness, and information. It is also the place where your soul colour shows most brightly in your energy fields. This soul colour holds amazing coding, and I believe it is the magnificent, sparkling vibrancy of this soul colour band in your energy fields that babies are deeply drawn to.

So you were born with this totally natural ability to see energy, and not only see it, but perceive energetic understandings through all of your senses and all of your own energy fields, even your skin. But unless you grew up in an exceptional household, this natural ability would not have been supported; it would not have been part of your shared experience with your family or your school mates. And because of this, your natural ability would have gradually been replaced by interpreting what you could see with your physical eyes and processing this information through your rational brain.

But our societal norms are full of experiences of perceiving energy, and you do it *all the time*. You just don't have the language for it.

What about when a friend walks into a café, for example, and you notice immediately that there is something wrong with them? Yes, in part, you are observing this on a physical level, based on how they are walking and their body language, and this is how your natural ability can rationally be understood. But you also know what your friend's energy fields look or feel like when they are vibrant and joyful and what they look like when they are upset or constricted.

What about when you just have a feeling about something, a hunch, perhaps about a job, a friendship, a health decision, or which way you should go in the car if you have two choices? Or perhaps you have a gut feeling about what your kids are about to do and whether it is going to be a good idea or a total disaster.

What about when you hold your baby or a beloved animal and you feel a deep and powerful sense of connection and love flowing between you? Or when you go to a party, a bar, or somewhere for dinner and you just feel really out of place or uncomfortable because it is too much for your energy systems or the energy of the place feels all wrong? What about when your partner is very stressed or angry about something, and you can be in a different room and feel that energy through the whole house? Or when you listen to music or dance and that amazing feel-good feeling gives you the tingles all over? For some people, just being in the presence of someone else who is feeling emotional and crying can make them feel the same way. Others can sense when their children or partner are nearly home or are coming up the steps a few minutes before they walk through the door.

All these are examples of when you perceive energy and are in direct and active communication with the wisdom of your own energy fields.

I have taught energy perception to hundreds of people. I give them paper and pencils and ask them to draw the energy fields of someone else. Once they stop feeling convinced that they can't perceive energy, presto! They can draw the energy fields in front of them very effectively. The biggest part of learning to perceive energy is *unlearning* that you can't!

Your entire energy system is in a continual exchange of information both internally and externally. You are always connected to the world around you.

Let's look at another example. Have you ever just had that sense that someone is watching you as you walk down the street and then finally look over your shoulder to see someone quickly looking away? That wasn't body language. That can't be explained away rationally or logically. That was your energy system experiencing an enquiry from another energy system, registering it, and informing your whole being. You are designed to be connected to everything around you, to be aware of it, and on some level, to be in exchange with it. This is the same whether you are walking down the street, in the forest, or by the sea. You are part of this entire web of life, and an *essential* part at that.

Yet another example is when you fall in love with someone. That is not rational or logical; it is all about energy. It is so amazing to see people's energy fields when they are first falling in love with each other. There is an explosion of radiance, of colour, of weaving. Have you ever fallen in love? Do you remember how everything in the world was better, how the people who usually annoyed you suddenly didn't seem so annoying after all, how every cloud looked remarkable, and how the sunrises and sunsets were the best you had ever seen? Do you remember how you could thrive even if you weren't getting very much sleep? Energetically, there was a very simple reason for this shift in perspective: the immense radiance held in the depth of your energetic core had become more activated and was radiating throughout your entire body, your entire being. Amazing!

But I want to tell you something even more amazing.

That way of experiencing the joy and ease of life is your natural way of being. It is your birthright to feel radiant and connected. It is your natural way to feel joyful and unlimited, to find calm even with the stresses in your life.

Do you believe me? Perhaps not quite yet. But keep reading and you will. Your energy fields are the foundation of your health. Understanding how to support them means being able to support your physical health, your mental health, and your vitality.

PRACTICES

 Thinking:
Your Everyday Perception

Let your mind wander around your day or days. With no judgement of yourself and no attachment to doing it "right" or having logical understanding around it, get curious about what you have perceived energetically. Where did you "just have a feeling" about someone or something?

 Feeling:
Feeling into the Energy Around You

Wherever you are right now, look about you. Look at the space all around you. Take all the time you want to really look. Notice things that you haven't noticed before in this space. Now close your eyes and feel into the energy of this specific space. What words would you use to describe how the energy of this space *feels* (not how it looks)? Friendly? Congested? Sad? Supportive? Harmonious? Jangly?

 Doing:
The Container of YOU

This easy practice keeps your energy systems well-contained to help build resilience, prevent vulnerability, and avoid feeling negatively impacted by any energy you are surrounded by.

1. Bring your hands together and rub your palms vigorously. You will probably feel some heat in your hands as you activate the energy centres in your palms.

2. Bring both hands to the centre of your chest, resting them one on top of the other. Think about, feel, and experience the heat from your hands moving into your heart area. Take three breaths (this is already a deeply healing and balancing practice).

3. From their position on your heart, push your arms straight out in front of you with the palms facing out, as if you are pushing away any stress or obstacles to your most beautiful life. When your arms are fully extended, your palms will be at the edge of your own energy field or biofield.

4. Think about, visualise, and imagine yourself inside the bubble of your own energy.

5. Pat the edge of your energy with your palms, with the intention of creating a strong, resilient, elastic edge all around you. This strong membrane can let in anything that is beneficial for your life and act as a buffer to anything that is not.

6. Continue to pat the edge of your energy field, all around your body (wherever you can reach, anyway!).

7. Bring your hands back to your heart centre, breathing in and out in the knowledge that you just helped create your strong and resilient energetic container.

The Container of You.

Remember, I have created videos of many of the practices in this book, so I can guide you as we do them together. You can find these videos and other supporting material at www.pruneharris.com/radiant-soul.

Everything that is in the heavens, on Earth, and under the Earth is penetrated with connectedness, penetrated with relatedness.

~Hildegard of Bingen
(1098–1179)

SHATTERING
THE ILLUSION
OF LIMITATION

How many people are trapped in their everyday habits: part numb, part frightened, part indifferent? To have a better life, we must keep choosing how we are living.

~Albert Einstein

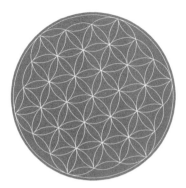

Your energy, and all that you are, is not a series of limitations. You are a vast bounty of limitless potential and possibility that is in emergence. If I gave you a magic wand that could transform three things about your life so you could get on with living the life you came here to live, what three things would you choose?

Unfortunately, I don't have that magic wand, yet when you can work to bring balance to your energy fields, then simple and powerful transformation is not so very far away.

I want to say something right here at the start of this chapter. I have worked with thousands of clients in clinical practice and have seen most of them undergo profound, empowered, and joyful changes in their lives. BUT! The quantity of change needed within their energy fields was remarkably small for such a big effect. It is often a simple understanding or sidestep from where you already are that will bring about significant results.

Don't think you have to understand everything about your energy fields to see much more ease, health, and vitality in your daily life. A slight shift in vibration, a small readjustment of a pattern that got stuck somewhere along the way, a tiny expansion that leads to full body alignment – that is what I want you to keep close to your heart and mind as you read this. Tiny changes in your energy fields can bring profound changes to how you feel in your everyday life.

JUST LIKE RIDING A BIKE

Imagine that you are cycling on a two-metre-wide path. Half of the path is stable, smooth, and constant, a quarter of the path has gravel and bumps on it, and the other quarter is pitted and boggy with edges against a sheer drop. As you cycle along the smooth path, if you start straying towards the gravel-covered part of it, all you have to do is slightly adjust the weight of your body and make a tiny movement to your handlebars, and your bike moves over to the smooth side of the path again. Easy and simple because you know how to adjust your body or the handlebars. But what if you didn't know how?

I learned how to ride a bike when I was young, but never did it very much. One day, a 15-year-old friend with two mopeds suggested we go along the lane for a bit of fun. Well, I was

←————————

Tiny changes in your energy fields can bring profound changes to how you feel in your everyday life.

up for it – until I got to the first sharp corner and tried to turn, not by moving the handlebars from left to right, but by moving the handlebars up and over as if they were a steering wheel. Needless to say, I went straight into the hedge and fell off! And yet it is so obvious, isn't it? Just turn the handlebars to the left or right to go around the corner (not my proudest moment). My point here is that balancing your energy fields is also simple, easy, and obvious when you know how to do it!

Just to take this cycling analogy a little further, what if you have only ever been cycling on the gravel and bumps or, worse, slogging through recent years in the pitted bog, getting stuck and terrified that the sheer drop is always present? If you have been experiencing these kinds of challenges in your life, I know you have been trying your hardest to do everything you can do to get your life back on track, thinking, *Surely it doesn't have to be this hard?* You have been bringing all of your commitment and determination to get yourself sorted out physically and emotionally, for yourself and for all of your relationships.

No one *chooses* to be bumping along, reactive, and uncertain. No one *chooses* to struggle in their life. Whatever challenges you may be experiencing right now are not the result of a conscious choice you made willingly and fully informed of all of your options.

I know you have been doing all you can, because experience and energy have taught me that everyone always does the very best they can do in the circumstances they are in. And I know you are deeply committed to this, because you have reached for a book to help you experience a fuller, better, more empowered and joyful life. You possibly have a desire to be a better you.

But I want to tell you, you already *are* the better you. There are just some old habits in your energy fields that are holding you back from being able to deeply experience the joy and ease of your own life – habits based on your life experiences that are now being held within your energy fields. These habits are all about survival. They are wise and amazing . . . and totally outdated. They came into your awareness when you were growing up, and if your memory of your childhood is that it was fun, awesome, and empowering, then your energy systems are likely in much more cohesion than if you remember it as being challenging, painful, embarrassing, and thoroughly unbalanced!

YOUR PHYSICAL BODY IS GOVERNED BY YOUR ENERGY BODY

Every one of your energy systems fits together perfectly to flow from one to the other, receiving information from each other and adjusting patterns accordingly. What is really important to understand about the human energy system at this point is that it governs your physical body. It is the human energy system that holds the blueprint of your physical health, your resilience, your radiance, and your ability to adjust to life's road.

This is a very cool understanding, and one that the modern medical model has not yet caught up with. But I am quite sure that it will, and you are part of leading this change in health consciousness.

Have you ever noticed that when you are feeling vibrant, happy, and engaged with life, you never get ill, even if the flu is hitting every member of your family? Your energy system protects you, and when you are in your vital and harmonious energy, your physical body will be kept in that very same place.

Now let's take a different example. Have you ever noticed when you have had a headache that you were already feeling stressed or out of sorts beforehand? I doubt you have been struck by a headache on the days you felt amazing, vital, and vibrant; it just doesn't work like that. You developed a headache because your energy system was already a bit off.

Your physical body manifests the imbalance in your energy system as physical symptoms. Everything that you experience with your health and in your body has already been present in your energy system for a while. And if you have chronic physical conditions such as migraines, IBS, recurring slipped discs, or autoimmune diseases, then these energy patterns have been in your system for a *long* time.

Everything that you experience is already held in your energy patterns. When you learn to adjust those patterns and return them to balance, you can truly and deeply heal your physical body, balance your emotions, and change your interaction with your own life.

Every moment of every day, your energy is the first place you experience your world. If, when you wake up, you are feeling a bit vulnerable, that is because a pattern in your protective energy system isn't quite holding. If you know how to shift and manage that energy system, you can quite literally change your life and how you experience it. And *that* is why I am writing this book. You are very, very powerful. You have 100 percent, complete control over your personal world and worldview. That is not to say that you can control other people in your life, the fact that the train is late, or that your dog chewed up your tax return. But it does mean that in any situation, you can choose how you feel and how you respond. And I mean truly choose. Not just *try* to choose.

You may have studied meditation or mindfulness and have the great skills that those practices bring into your life, yet you can still fall into old patterns of dysfunction when push comes to shove. Through repetition, meditation, and mindfulness techniques, you can help train your energy systems back towards greater balance and cohesion. Beautiful! But how easy is it for you to access this peace and bliss when you are in the middle of a stressful situation?

The adage of 'just think positive' feels to me like a very good marketing tagline, but it isn't always helpful or even possible, especially when we are caught in a difficult or stressful situation. Thinking positive does help raise your awareness that a pattern of thought or emotion needs to change, but rarely does it change the pattern itself. This is because the patterns that you revert to are held not in your brain, but in your energy fields. When you are able to clear and balance these patterns in your energy systems through energy interventions, you can truly choose your responses to every situation.

This makes you immensely powerful.

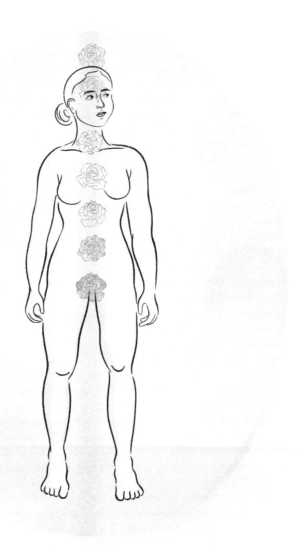

Your energy system is designed to align in connective cohesion to empower you throughout your life.

From this place of empowerment, you can choose to feel peace, calm, joy, and inspiration in all situations. You can have a beaming smile like the Dalai Lama, even in the middle of a life challenge. And I really mean it. You can. You just need to know how your energy systems work and how to fix the glitches your life has presented you with.

WEAVING IT TOGETHER

There are three distinct vibrations in every part of your energy anatomy (and we will get to explore just what energy systems make up your energy anatomy in the next few chapters). The three vibrations show up differently depending on what is going on in your energy systems and how they interface with your awareness or mind. This is the 'mind' in mindfulness, meaning the awareness process that is continually occurring between your thoughts and emotions, your energy and your physicality. The three vibrations are the functional, the creative, and the habitual.

The Functional Field

There are many processes in your physical body that are simply automatic and self-functional. You don't have to make your heart beat; it just does. You don't have to perform an action to make your lungs bring in oxygen or release carbon dioxide; they just do. There are countless processes in your physical body, and therefore in your energy fields, that exist as part of the whole with no consciousness necessary to function. The same is true for your energy fields. The chakras know where to be positioned and how to move. The aura knows to emanate from your body and surround it. In the upcoming chapters, you will learn more about the functions and purpose of each of these systems, but essentially this functional energy flow exists in all parts of your energy systems and all of your physicality. It exists and governs while you are developing in the womb and continues to maintain this functional field every moment of your life whether you are awake, asleep, acting consciously, or playing out a narrative from your subconscious.

The Creative Field

Every time you are actively engaged in being conscious, a specific vibration comes into your energy field. This is your creative vibration. 'Consciousness' can be defined as your awareness of your own internal states and the events going on around you. Energetically, consciousness means active engagement with the relational aspect of every part of your life. It means you don't just automatically react with a specific habitual action, thought, or emotion; you choose how to respond rather than react out of habit. This is the difference between engaging with the conscious parts of your mind, energy, and life and simply allowing your programmed habits to walk through life for you, as if you are walking in your sleep or in a trance.

Linked to your consciousness, the creative vibration is responsive, connective, and, well, creative!

The Habitual Field

Yep, you guessed it. The habitual field shows up in your energy systems when you are simply acting on habit. You aren't consciously engaging with your thoughts, emotions, or actions, you are just thinking, feeling, and doing them because that is what you do.

'It's who I am;' 'It's what I do;' 'It is what it is.' Oh, my heart saddens just thinking of these sayings, for so often they house resignation, despair, and a great big 'full stop' at the end of the sentence. They demonstrate no creativity, no exploration, and no curiosity about why you have just said what you said, thought what you thought, or felt what you felt. The habitual vibrational field begins to activate around areas of imbalance that can't be reconciled within the fullest functioning of your creative energy fields.

Linked to your subconscious, the habitual field is reactive, defensive, and habitual.

Babies are born with their creative fields buzzing and vibrating, while there is very little action in the habitual field. Slowly though, they become used to specific routines, specific ways of doing things, and especially specific understandings about the expectations of important others in their lives. They begin to learn what they should and shouldn't do and what they should and shouldn't be. Learning all the 'norms' of their social interactions is culturally essential for them. But what if these 'norms' don't light them up, let them shine, or even encourage them on their amazing and unique paths of becoming? What if the expectant 'norms' make them feel less – less worthy, less magnificent, less intelligent, less beautiful . . . less everything? This feeling is the slow and insidious creeping in of the habitual field that strengthens its programming, getting more and more programmed, until about your mid-30s. That is when there tends to be a big movement in all of your energy and you begin to reassess just exactly who you are, and maybe what you really want to be doing when you grow up! This self-exploration reignites the creative field and begins to reprogramme and dissolve the active habitual field around that specific topic or issue in your life.

So why can't you just decide to engage only in the creative field rather than the habitual? Well, you can, but it isn't quite that easy, and it has everything to do with the processing speed of your habitual and creative fields. You are an amazingly intricate, complex being. Your energy systems govern your physical body, while your consciousness forms the bridge between the two. And remember, your mind is not your brain. Your mind is the dance between your energy systems and the innate wisdom of your physical body, including your brain.

The challenge with engaging the creative field is that your conscious mind is much slower; you need to think about things and respond! Scientifically, your conscious mind operates at 40 bits of data per second, compared to your subconscious mind which, while operating at 40 million bits of data per second, is a million times quicker than your conscious thoughts. BUT! Your conscious mind, your creative energy, is hard wired into the energy of your soul. This means that it is powered by speed, light, vibration, and energy that can generate lightning-quick assessments of any situation and help you choose the creative option – the consciousness of potential in every interaction, every exchange, every thought, every moment. And this is great news! When you understand more about your energy systems and how you can move between the reactive habitual field into the responsive creative field, you have more choice every minute of every day. Old stresses and old habits no longer govern you, and this means being free from old programmes of dysfunction. You get to choose how to be you.

WHY WOULD YOUR ENERGY BE MOVING IN PATTERNS OF DYSFUNCTION IN THE FIRST PLACE?

Sometimes when you get stressed, overtired, or overwhelmed by the demands of your day, your energy patterns can lose their regular healthy flow and begin holding patterns of dysfunction instead. The patterns start to unravel and, little by little, your energy cohesion and organisation unravel too. If you are able to rest, sleep, practice, have fun, or do whatever you need to do to return to your balance, then these processes will help restore the healthy pattern and flow to your energy systems. BUT! When you experience stress, tiredness, or overwhelm day after day for a prolonged period of time, your energy systems can begin holding a chronic pattern of imbalance that can become deeply embedded in the habitual field. This will most likely result in emotional turmoil, ill health, or disease.

The connectiveness and cohesion of your energy system is deeply affected by stressful situations.

Let's think about what stressful situations *might* just crop up:

- Relationship tension – with your mum, dad, child, spouse, lover, boss, neighbour . . . an inexhaustible list of every relationship possible.

- Financial worry – no explanation necessary. It is universally applicable, even at very different levels of financial need.

- Career or job worry – fear of losing your job, dissatisfaction with your career, frustration at hitting a glass ceiling for cultural or gender reasons, or relationship conflict at work.

- Ill health – yours or loved ones, including cancer, heart disease, autoimmune illnesses . . . the list goes on. Chronically ill health of any kind can be defined as a stressful situation.

- Cultural strife and divisiveness in your community or country – such as the current political chaos.

- Strife and divisiveness across the globe – watching the news can be deeply stressful and set in motion a wave of futility that can flood your entire system.

- The current environmental crisis – we are all experiencing and involved with this in some way, whether we are helping, avoiding, feeling overwhelmed with, or ignoring it.

- Living – daily life can be a wheel of movement from the minute the alarm demands you get out of bed until you drop back into bed again, with the niggling feeling that you now have more on your to-do list than you had when you woke up.

The important take-home message here is that dysfunction is always apparent in the energy systems before it gets through to the body. It is just basic physics that the subtlest energies will be affected by other energy before the densest energies will respond. So your subtle energy systems in your aura will show up as imbalance long before they have solidified into ill health in your body. The *great* news is that you can do something about these energy patterns. Easily. Simply. One day in the future, understanding of essential energy will be taught in the home and at school. I am convinced of it. When enough people understand just how powerful they can be at affecting their own balance, health, and vitality, it will become the new normal.

IT IS YOUR BIRTHRIGHT TO FEEL AMAZING!

How do you feel when your energy is coherent? Amazing! (Whatever your own personal version of amazing is.) When your energy systems are in coherence, you can experience joy, stability, and mental clarity, as well as easy connection to people, animals, and the world around you. You can keep your balance when someone or something throws a curveball into your day, and you can even keep your sense of humour. You feel expansive and trusting and can deeply engage with your own life. You feel like you belong (because you do).

I really, really hope you have experienced times in your life when you felt this way. You have a birthright to feel this balanced, connected, and happy.

I am also pretty sure that you have experienced the opposite of energetic coherence and been crippled with emotion or overwhelm. Maybe you have felt lonely, desperate, angry, depressed, stuck in a mind fog, frightened to take the next step of growth in your life, untrusting, or unsafe. And I know you have felt disconnected from others and from your own personal

————————▶

You have a birthright to feel balanced, connected and happy.

power and joy, but that is because you didn't have the tools to make the gentle, subtle shifts to your energy that were needed during that time.

It is my intention that once you have read this book, you will have effective, gentle, and powerful tools to support you as you walk your own essential path. Because remember, you often need only the tiniest shift in your energy fields to bring about expansive blossoming from experiencing an issue or problem that is held in your habitual field to something that can flourish in your creative field. This may be a physical symptom, such as a bad back or cancer, an emotional symptom, such as not being able to fully commit to a relationship, or a cosmic symptom, such as a feeling you don't belong or there is no purpose to your life. All these symptoms are caused by an energetic imbalance. To heal fully, you simply need to activate the energetic bridge in your amazing and creative system. How? We are going to get to that in the next few chapters, but essentially anything can activate and trigger this healing movement! Or rather, anything you do with consciousness. To bring transformation into your life, you need to think, feel, or do something to help create this bridge and begin to thrive.

The next seven chapters are your toolkit for understanding your energy anatomy and bringing transformation into your life. Your tool kit may contain energy practices, consciousness practices, time to think about things, and conscious actions, for these tools create energy bridges between every part of your energy anatomy. They induce that shift from moving through your life habitually, reactively, or functionally, to being able to flourish and respond in the co-creative dance of your life.

PRACTICES

Thinking:
Seeing the Change

1. Take out a piece of paper and a pen and write down 10 things you would like to change about your life.

2. Now look at this list and choose the three changes that would bring about the most transformation for you.

3. What would this transformation look like? How would your life be different because of these changes?

Even simply getting *really* clear about what transformation you would like to invite into your life and why can help your energy coalesce around such a possibility. This helps align your intention and attention to empower the changes you wish to see in your own life and bring them into being.

Feeling:
The Gift of Your Body

Find a time when you can be undisturbed for a few minutes. Sit or lie down in the position where you feel most comfortable. I want you to really relax and not have to even support your body frame; that is what your bones are for! Take a few breaths and begin to bring your awareness to how you are feeling. So often, your to-do list can mean that you don't even get a chance to really feel into how you are, so that is what we are doing here. Each time you bring your awareness and ask the questions, *How is my body feeling? How am I feeling?*, you invite space into your energy fields and the potential for them to switch from the habitual to the creative field.

For some people, finding words to describe how they are feeling is really easy, and for others, it is very difficult, so here is a short list of feelings to help guide you.

Tense, relaxed, tight, happy, angry, grumpy, hurt, sore, joyful, stressed, expansive, tired, nourished, loved, alone, odd, uncertain, confident, full, empty, grateful.

As you take this time to explore how you are feeling, if you want to support your whole body system process and balance even more deeply, then move on to the 'Doing' practice below.

 Doing:
Coming Home to Yourself

In the upcoming chapters, you will learn many practices to help you evolve your energy systems away from the habitual and towards the creative. This is one of the simplest and most powerful techniques that begins to stabilise all of your energy fields and helps you come home to yourself, in all of your magnificent potential. Use it anytime you feel stressed or off balance.

1. Place the palm and fingers of one hand gently on your forehead.

2. Place the other hand flat on your belly, below your navel.

3. Take a few nourishing breaths. Your hands are connecting essential energy flows in your body that will help you to be more resilient.

4. If it feels good for you, finish by placing both of your hands over your heart centre.

Remember, I have created videos of many of the practices in this book, so I can guide you as we do them together. You can find these videos and other supporting material at www.pruneharris.com/radiant-soul.

You cannot get through a single day without having an impact on the world around you. What you do makes a difference, and you have to decide what kind of a difference you want to make.

~Jane Goodall
(1934–present)

3

UNDERSTAND YOUR ENERGY, UNDERSTAND YOUR LIFE

Peace comes through understanding.

~Albert Einstein

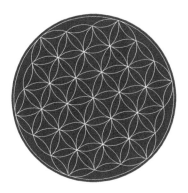

When I was 11 and in my last year of primary school, I played the lead role in a musical. Although not a natural performer, I could hold a tune, and it felt just fine to play a 21-year-old pirate called Frederick. It didn't occur to me to question my ability to do it, because the teacher thought I could and I was happy to trust that – until dress rehearsal day when my voice cracked as I sang a note and my classmates laughed at me. It was harmless laughter, not malicious, they just thought it was funny that my voice cracked. But it changed my world. From that point on, I was increasingly terrified to speak up in front of any group of people.

The older I got, the more entrenched this fear became. Even *thinking* of saying something would make my heart start beating like crazy, my face flush red, and my entire body start shaking. While I was at university, it took immense courage simply to speak up in class. I oscillated between telling myself it was crazy to worry about saying what I wanted to say and feeling terror that would hit me physically any time I thought about doing it! A deeply internal process, it was pretty miserable, and because it was so deeply entrenched in my habitual vibrational field, it hit many of my energy systems as well. I couldn't find a way to change this old and horribly limiting pattern, even though I could watch what was unravelling and locking up within my own system. I felt squished in my own life, as though I couldn't communicate who I really was, because something was blocking me from doing so.

When I did finally understand how to shift my energy, it took less than 20 minutes for me to clear this old glitchy programme of embarrassment and fear out of my system and help it return in balance with my creative vibrational field. There was *nothing* holding it in place, nothing that was attached to keeping it part of the status quo. It was simply a glitch, a programme, a habit that was running on repeat every time I wanted to say something to a group of more than about four people.

What did I do to change that hugely limiting and restrictive fear? How did I dissolve that aspect of my habitual field?

I reprogrammed my chakras. I connected the places in my energy system that kept pressing the repeat button on that old story. This old pattern was especially sitting in my throat

→

Your chakras hold energetic information about every experience you have had during your life.

chakra (expression), my third chakra (personal identity), and my second chakra (innocence).

Will this work for you? Possibly. And I want to explain more here.

When I write 'Understand your energy, understand your life,' I mean it. For me, this limiting imbalance was sitting in my chakras. For you, it might be sitting in your chakras, your aura, or your meridians. When you have a basic understanding of your energy systems, you are empowered to bring about all the change you wish to see.

There are three simple steps to using your own energy to heal whatever isn't working in your life, which may include your physical health, emotional turmoil or disconnection, or simply the feeling that you aren't quite living the life that you are *meant* to be living:

Step 1: Know the basic anatomy of your amazing energy system and how it supports and connects everything about you.

Step 2: Learn how to tell whether these systems are in balance or out of balance and whether they hold patterns of health or disturbance and disease.

Step 3: Apply the simple activities or practices to repattern, nurture, and evolve your energy so you have choices in every situation.

In the next seven chapters, we are going to explore your basic energy anatomy in more detail so that you can be empowered to make the choices that are right for you, your physical health, and your emotional and mental health, as well as for the health and nurturing of all your potential.

Your energy anatomy encompasses six energy systems:

1. The energetic core.

2. The aura or biofield.

3. The elemental rhythms.

4. The energy channels.

5. The chakras.

6. The heartfield.

Each one of these systems could be the topic of a book itself, so as we move forward from here, I am going to be weaving in and out of how these immense, complex, and beautiful aspects of your energy anatomy affect your everyday life.

All energy systems are interconnected, yet have different vibrations. Think of your physical body; you have a body that you can consider a whole, and you have individual parts of that whole such as your arm, your leg, your eye, and your liver. Each looks very different and has a specific and unchangeable function, yet together, they form your one whole body. It is the same with your energy systems. Your chakras are quite different from your aura, and your heartfield is totally different

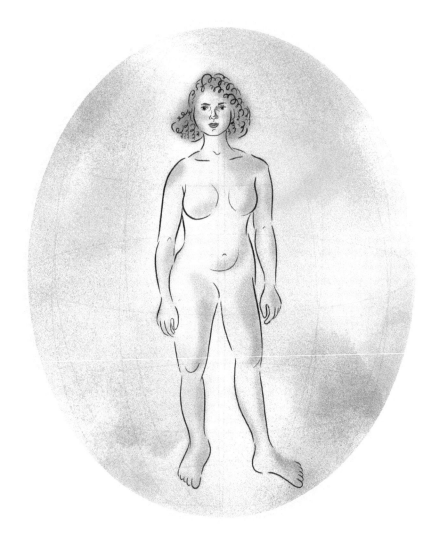

Understand your energy, understand your life.

from your meridian system. They each look different and have a specific and unchangeable function, yet together they form your human energy anatomy system.

It really is mind-blowingly beautiful to watch the way human energy fields move in constant patterns of unfolding and enfolding – huge patterns, tiny patterns, patterns that weave all the different aspects together even as they hold specific and separate vibrations within the whole. You are literally hardwired for balance, health, cohesion, and interconnectiveness at every level.

So let's start exploring these energy systems, beginning with the deepest and most essential one you have: the energetic core.

Wisdom is sweeter than honey,

brings more joy than wine,

illumines more than the sun,

is more precious than jewels.

~Makeda, Queen of Sheba

(ca. 1000 BC)

THE ENERGETIC
CORE

The soul given to each of us is moved by the same living spirit that moves the universe.

~Albert Einstein

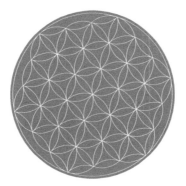

Deep in the core of your body is an energy system that defines everything about you. It is the energy of the centre of your being, and from that deep place within travels through every single cell in your body, every thought in your mind, every emotion in your heart, out through your skin, and all the way through your biofield.

You can think of this *energetic core* running through the very centre of you, following the line of your spine, with start and end points above the centre of your head and below the centre of your feet. Energy flows into your body from both above and below to nourish this vital essential energy, which we could also describe as the energy of your soul.

Have you ever wondered what your soul looks like, where it lives, how it is attached to you, or just what a 'soul' is? How much is your soul you? How much are you your soul? I am no theologian or philosopher, but I do know energy, and since I was tiny, the one system that was always the most apparent to me (way before I understood about meridians, chakras, dantians, or the components of the biofield) was the energy of the soul.

Mostly, this energy is so apparent because it is the brightest, lightest, highest vibration and is totally inseparable from the person. It shines through every other energy within and around that person. But before I can best explain it to you, first, a story.

I was standing in my kitchen with my husband, watching a nine-year-old friend of my son's walk up the drive. As he walked by the window, I said to my husband, 'It's amazing how this little guy's light shines so brightly, isn't it?'

He looked at me and said, 'You know I don't see energy.'

'I know, but you see that?' I asked, turning to him.

'No,' he answered.

I was astounded. In fact, I didn't believe him. 'You see that light he follows just in front of his chest? That really bright soul light?'

'No, I don't,' he answered.

I don't think I said anything for many, many minutes. I was processing this information, and the dawning understanding was reshaping my entire world. I was 36 years old.

I grilled my husband mercilessly over the next few hours about what exactly he saw, and then I asked friends and family members, until I gradually built up a picture of a vastly different world than the one I was used to inhabiting. A world where

The conversation about that little boy's assemblage point changed my life.

people navigated mainly through awareness of the physical world (which has the densest and slowest matter).

Your amazing, beautiful body plays out the tune your energy fields create, and at the deepest parts of your energy fields, at your energetic core, is the energy of your soul. You have specific energy anatomy to house this immense and essential soul energy and help it be both connected and protected. This soul energy has two distinctive vibrations. The first is the *Core Soul*, which is the deepest energy that runs within your energetic core and connects above and below. The second is the *Radiant Soul*, which flows from the *Core Soul* through all that you are at a physical and energetic level.

I want to say right here and now that I have never seen a soul energy that is 'bad' or 'evil' or even corrupted in any way. Your soul light shines brightly, just as my and every person's soul light shines brightly. When a baby is born, their soul light is just as strong as an adult's. And just before someone transitions into death, their soul light is incredibly bright, no matter what kind of life they have led.

At the core of everyone is connection, brilliance, and cosmic truth.

A MODERN-DAY VERSION OF SOS!

There are also, of course, habits and patterns that we grow into as we move through our lives. Some are life-affirming, soul-affirming patterns that enhance every aspect of our lives; they exist within the creative vibration of our energy fields. Others may be life-restricting or even soul-shattering. If we engage in these patterns over and over, our access to our soul energy and wisdom can diminish as we experience power loss and even soul loss. This is quite common in our modern-day lives where we don't really have the language around soul care. Our modern cultures place ever-greater emphasis on how to care for individual and societal mental health as well

→

Your energetic core is a superhighway of light filaments, weaving in a dance of your uniqueness, yet also inseparable from the energy that comes from the Earth and the Cosmos.

as our physical health. And with both of those essential and foundational increases in awareness, we can now reach the deepest level of human awareness and ask, 'How do we care for our souls?' We need to remodel the old SOS code into a daily call, a daily awareness, of 'Save Our Souls!' Knowing how your energy fields house this soul energy and how you can nurture it is a good start to taking care of all that you are in your magnificence and beauty.

For centuries, the Chinese have named this core energy 'the Taiji Pole,' and the ancient Indians called it the 'Sushumna Nadi.' If you need practical visuals, then think of an energetic hosepipe running through the centre of your body (I know it isn't a glamorous image, but it works!). During some of my classes, my clients and I change 'energetic hosepipe' to 'crystalline channel,' but we always come back to agreeing that the hosepipe analogy works and is easy to understand.

This hosepipe is the structure that houses the soul energy that is continually flowing through it. It is where the world's soul touches the energy of your *Core Soul* as it connects to the Cosmos above and the Earth below.

THE CORE SOUL

Through your *Core Soul*, which is quintessentially and uniquely yours, you are connected to all of creation. At this soul level, you know your true worth and the truth that you are priceless and essential in every way. You know that just as a stone deserves to exist, so do you. Just as an elephant deserves harmony and health, so do you. Just as the happiest person you know deserves happiness, so do you.

And at this soul level, you know the truth of the universe. No smart marketing or political spin can baffle or bamboozle this truth metre.

When I look at this level in the human energy system, it blows me away. And I don't quite know if I can do it justice through words. Think of the most beautiful thing you have ever seen. Perhaps it is your newborn baby, the most soul-touching sunset, or seeing your beloved after a long time apart. Now, describe what you see in words in a way that actually does it justice. Tricky, isn't it? Because mostly what you 'see' is the *feeling* you have when you 'see' it. Otherwise, you would simply say, 'I am looking at a baby with a little snub nose, a squished face, milky eyes, tiny fingers . . . ' Instead, (thinking of my own babies being born) it is a little more like this: *I am looking at perfection – overwhelming, explosive perfection – and I don't know how to feel anything this big. She is perfect, and she has a nose, and look at those fingers; they are perfect! How can anything be so perfect and tiny and yet so huge? I'm terrified, and she is perfect. And the joy is bigger than this entire hospital. In fact, it is bigger than the whole world. This baby is my baby, and she is so perfect.* Well, writing about the human soul energy is a bit like this, because, of course, when that little baby is in your arms for the first time, you *are* meeting their soul and experiencing their soul in its human form. That is why it feels so big and beyond words.

So, while I can describe what the human energetic core looks like, I don't think I can express to you its sheer power and beauty or the way in which it has both an essential human feel and a stellar/cosmic energy that runs through it. But let's have a go!

Your energetic core is a superhighway of light filaments, weaving in a dance of your uniqueness, yet also inseparable from the energy that comes from the Earth and the Cosmos. Energy runs through this energetic core both ways, from above to below, and from below to above. Often, gold or silver filaments super-speed through this energetic core. For *Star Trek* fans, think of the visual that accompanies warp speed; for *Star Wars* fans, think light speed; and for Marvel and *Thor* fans, think of the Bifrost that links Asgard to Midgard!

Your sun star is a powerful energy centre that connects you with all that is above.

A metre or so above your head is an energy centre that heralds the top of your energetic core. This is the *Sun star*. It is a powerful energy centre that connects you with all that is above. Likewise, about a metre below your feet is a powerful energy centre that connects you with the Earth beneath your feet. This is the *Earth star*. You can think of the *Sun star* and the *Earth star* as the interface points between your human energy and the energy from the Earth and the Cosmos.

Through your energetic core, your *Core Soul* energy meets the world around you through the *Sun star* and the *Earth star*. When those powerful energy hubs aren't connecting well, you can feel cut off from your support or inspiration. You can feel like you are alone or drifting through your life with little inspired

The Earth Star is a powerful energy centre that connects you with the Earth beneath your feet.

purpose. When those energy hubs are active, connected, and vital, then that is exactly how *you* feel. From this place of connection and flow, you move through your world feeling guided and able to truly be present in the choices and the grace of your life. The world effortlessly moves around and within you. For those of you who feel better when you connect to nature, this is a huge part of *why* you feel better when you are outside. Being outside, without hustle and bustle, can help reconnect both your *Earth star* and your *Sun star* and strengthen their natural ways of being. This means you can be resourced much more deeply as you become more of a conduit for energy to flow through you from above to below and from below to above. As this energy flow moves through your energetic core, you become resourced and refreshed from relaxing, enlivening, and connecting your *Core Soul* to its place within the grander cosmic energy.

Within your *Core Soul* superhighway is a continual flow of cosmic coding as well as the essential human parts of you. Your energetic core holds the interface for how this cosmic coding will be expressed in the individual package of your human life. It doesn't in any way give a predetermined life path (the universe holds far too much chaos for that!), but all knowledge of creation is continually running through your core, connecting 'you' to the cosmic vastness of the universe. There is nothing electromagnetic about the energy that is super-speeding through your energetic core. This is light energy, subtle energy, the radiance that you see pour from some people and concealed in others. Your body, however, is hugely electromagnetic, and hopefully it does the wonderful job of keeping you physically grounded while this superhighway of cosmic and human soul energy whizzes through your core.

Where the super-soul highway meets the edge of the energetic core, there is an interface of immense potential. That is the tamest way I have ever expressed it. If you asked me in person what it looked like, I would burst into a passionate and enthusiastic description. Have you seen a picture of a nebula taken through a super high-powered telescope? Go ahead and try to use words to describe it in all its vastness and magnificence. What might you say? The image is magical, mystical, mind-blowing, and so rich with potential that even the words 'rich with potential' fall flat. Well, that is what this interface looks like: your personal and unique nebula formation. This is where your *Core Soul* meets your physical body in all its wonder and flows through your entire body as the *Radiant Soul*.

This *Radiant Soul* energy flows through every part of your physicality, every part of your emotional and cognitive systems, every part of your everything connecting you to yourself, others, the planet, and the Cosmos.

I remember so clearly the first time I ever worked clinically to balance the energetic core with a client.

Bea turned up in my clinic with a lot of joy and a happy life, which is how she described herself. She was a holistic practitioner and wanted an 'energetic tune up,' and since she had heard of me, she came in to have a session.

And she was right. Joy was rolling through her energy system, her smile was huge enough to fill a room, and she emanated kindness. Yet, when I looked at her system, it was as if there was an emptiness somewhere, an absence. The rest of her systems were leaping and jumping to bridge the absence, but there it was. The more I tracked it, the more I could see it. The energy of her *Core Soul* was magnificent and vibrant, but the interface between her *Core Soul* and her *Radiant Soul* was shattered. There is no other word for it. The energy was shattered into a million tiny fragments that were very close to each other and all in the right places, but no longer forming a whole. Bea's 'hosepipe' was broken. Each individual piece shone with the exquisiteness of core energy, but they were all stuck like a million tiny diamonds spinning in one place. I also found that my own chest felt like it had been struck hard, and I could feel the grief and inability to breathe.

OK, if we worked with this, this was no 'tune up.'

When I asked Bea whether she had experienced a loss or significant grief in her life, she looked at me and her energy shifted. The strength that came through her aura was like steel wires reaching from her core, supporting her heart, grounding her deeply, and holding her strong.

'Yes,' she said, 'My son. He died in my arms in a road traffic accident.' Still, the steel wires carried strength, energy, and vitality to her entire system.

'I think there is a small part of your system that is still looking for healing around that loss, Bea. I can see that you have healed so much, so beautifully, that you have so much strength, and that your amazing desire to live is connecting so much.'

'I had to be strong for my other children. The ones who were left; the ones who are still here,' she responded.

After we talked more, Bea chose to work on healing that interface in her energetic core. I explained that work at that level required time for integration and that perhaps we should schedule it for a time when she had a few restful days planned. Then we laughed at the 'coincidence' that just that morning she had cancelled her clients for the rest of the week and decided to spend time in her garden. The Cosmos was supporting her healing!

Connecting to the energy of her *Sun star* and *Earth star*, I worked to invite the interface of her *Core* and *Radiant Soul* energy to return to the pattern of balance that it had known before the immense trauma and shock of her son's death. Slowly, those tiny shattered pieces began to move together, spinning, moving, beginning to weave. Within 30 minutes, they found their way into wholeness, and then the energy that flowed through her system was immense, beautiful, and gentle. It was a homecoming as she became more whole, more her. I never saw the energy that looked like steel wires in her energy field again. She no longer needed that level of willpower and determined strength.

I have worked hundreds of times now helping people balance their energetic core and find true energetic connection, and each time is a marvel and the deepest, deepest honour.

YOUR SOUL COLOUR

The vibration of your *Core Soul* is represented in a colour. Colour is simply a vibration, so the vibration of green is different from the vibration of blue, and that is why we perceive them as different colours. Your *Radiant Soul* has a colour that is unique to you; you could call it your *soul colour* or life colour. Every

Your *Radiant Soul* energy flows through every part of your physicality, every part of your emotional and cognitive systems, every part of your everything connecting you to yourself, others, the planet, and the Cosmos.

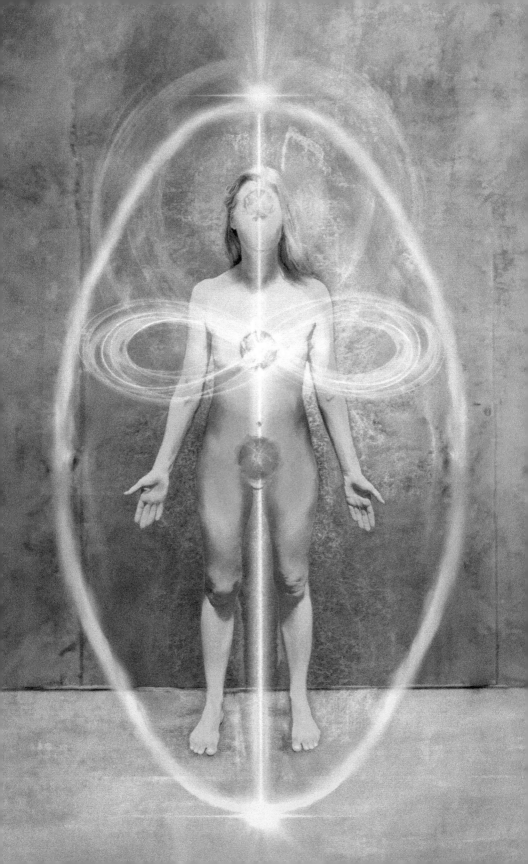

person has a *soul colour*. This *soul colour* helps illustrate the strengths and challenges you have at your depths.

If I were to look at you, I would see many layers of varying colours all expressing different emotions and themes. Remember, colours are only vibrations, so there is a different vibration for the emotion of love, the emotion of anger, the emotion of happiness, and so on. Your thoughts deeply affect your energy fields, so the colours will continually change depending on what you are thinking. Some of these colours may be moving, swirling, exploding, popping, spinning like a tornado, or dispersing like mist. Others may be quite still, showing up as a specific theme or a set pattern of emotions. Some of these colours or vibrations of energy, thought, and emotion are quite superficial and will quickly spark or whizz across your energy fields (think of a comet) as you have a quick burst of thought or emotion. You may experience this as a flash of irritation, a sudden humour, or simply a remembering of part of your shopping list. Other colours are a much more permanent part of your energetic whole.

There is also a difference in the vibration of the colour of your energy depending on whether it is your creative or habitual field that is relating that thought, emotion, or issue. Generally, the category of the colour is the same, but the hue or tone of it is quite different. Have you ever walked through grass on a sunlit, dewy morning and seen the green grass sparkling with the crystalline twinkling of the Sun? The colour of the grass is the same as it is later in the day when the dew has gone and the Sun is no longer activating that magical sparkle, but the vibration of the green is quite different, isn't it? The colours in your energy fields are the same way. When they are housed within your habitual and reactive energy fields, they look like grass without the sunlight and dew magic, as opposed to when they are being activated within the creative and responsive energy fields in your systems.

The deepest of these vibrations is the *soul colour*, as that colour begins in your energetic core and then emanates throughout your entire physical, energetic, emotional, and cognitive systems. Every cell you have is bathed in your *soul colour*. Your skin is resonant with your soul colour, and as it continues through the energy field that surrounds your physical body, your soul colour spreads out to the very edge of your aura. You are amazing.

PRACTICES

 Thinking:
What Does the Word 'Soul' Mean to You?

How would you describe your soul to a beloved listener? If you could think of a colour that you resonate with or in some way feels 'right' for your soul colour, what would it be?

 Feeling:
Greeting Your Sun Star

Sit comfortably and take three relaxing, nourishing breaths. Now raise both hands above your head with your arms stretched up and your elbows slightly bent. Place the fingertips of your hands together. Your hands will be resting around the energy hub of your *Sun star*, which is about the size of a large orange. Tune into the fact that you are holding this spherical energy hub in your hands. What does it feel like? How does it feel if you move your palms away from each other a little and then return to your fingertips touching? Keep playing, and observe how it feels as you support this area with your hands and your awareness.

 Doing:
The Breath of Your Life

Relax your body and bring awareness to your breath. Feel the breath coming in and out of your body and your body expanding and contracting in time with your breath. As you inhale, think or say, *I breathe the joy of life into my being*. As you exhale, think or say, *I breathe the joy of being into life*. Continue this for several breaths and, when you are ready, begin to allow your imagination and intention to carry the energy of your in-breath right into your energetic core. As you breathe out, allow this energy to flow from your core, throughout your body, towards your skin, through your skin, and into the energy that surrounds your body. Continue breathing this way, inviting core wisdom, ease, joy, and energy through every part of your being.

Remember, I have created videos of many of the practices in this book, so I can guide you as we do them together. You can find these videos and other supporting material at www. pruneharris.com/radiant-soul.

Perhaps there is a language which is not made of words and everything in the world understands it. Perhaps there is a soul hidden in everything and it can always speak, without even making a sound, to another soul.

~The Little Princess
by Frances Hodgson Burnett
(1849–1924)

5

THE AURA

What you can't imagine,

you can't discover.

~Albert Einstein

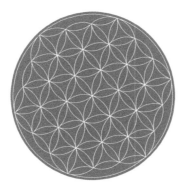

Your aura is amazing. It is splendiferous. It is mind-blowingly, jaw-droppingly fabulous. I wish, wish, wish you could see your own aura, as it is one of the most beautiful sights you will ever see.

Right now, your aura, also referred to as your *biofield*, is moving and swirling in patterns with every thought or emotion, sending streaks of colour, light, and movement through your entire energy field. It may be close to your body, snug and tight. It may be filling a space three metres off your body, emanating and radiating *you* into the room, garden, or park where you are reading this.

When your aura is vibrant, you feel vibrant. Simple as that. You feel protected, connected, and aware. This enables you to navigate through your world easily because you know yourself to be safe, trusting, and able to understand the seemingly

invisible cues that are all around you. You are always connected and protected.

When your aura is compromised, you can feel unsupported, vulnerable, and edgy. Because your aura is continually responding to every thought, every emotion, and every internal and external experience, it can lose some of its cohesion and connectiveness. When that happens, you also lose a lot of your natural energetic protection. When your physical body is weak, it is highly likely that your auric field will also be weak, for it is the electrical energy of your cells that fuels your auric field.

One of the most influential factors in auric compromise is unmanaged stress. The continued adrenal and cortisol fight–flight–freeze response demands too much of the physical and energetic resources that would otherwise go towards creating and nurturing the beautiful and tightly woven energy field around you.

When your aura is compromised, you can become much more susceptible to external pathogens as well as negatively impacted by other people's energy, words, and thoughts. Simply put, when your aura is not able to do its job effectively, you don't feel particularly safe, supported, or resilient. You feel that if something came along to give you a (metaphorical) shove, you would fall down, implode, or explode. Those days when you simply feel vulnerable or jangled to the point that

Your aura is created by the electrical and subtle energy fields powered from deep inside the electricity in every cell of your physical body.

The aura is one of the wisest parts of your entire system, for it is continually responding to every internal and external stimulus.

When your aura is compromised, you can become much more susceptible to external pathogens as well as negatively impacted by other people's energy, words, and thoughts.

everything feels edgy and uncertain? Those are days when your aura is compromised. Depending on what is going on for you, you may explode in a protective anger, collapse in a tearful puddle, or both, but you can do so much to help enhance and support your aura's natural vitality.

The aura is one of the wisest parts of your entire system, for it is continually responding to every internal and external stimulus. Perhaps you have seen colourful images of Kirlian photography. They are wonderful, they are accurate, and they are a tiny, tiny snapshot frozen in time of something that is vast, dynamic, and continually shifting.

When I first passed my driving test, I took to the roads like a girl racer. I drove everywhere as fast as I possibly could, and I *loved* it. I now drive slowly to enjoy the world as I pass through it, but as a teenager, my love of speeding drove me as I drove the car. One day, as I was careening in my little car alone through the tiny lanes of Cornwall, I was rather surprised to receive the information from my aura that there was someone sitting in the back seat. My energy fields let me know in the form of a gentle push, and I looked in the mirror to see a man in a flat cap sitting in the middle of the back seat. Have I already said that seeing those who have transitioned is part of my life? They are simply energy, after all. This friendly visitor sitting in the back seat of the car looked straight at me in the mirror and said, 'You need to pull over and stop. A car is coming around the next bend about as fast as you. You need to pull over and stop.' Well, as a teenager you may argue with some things, but not that! I pulled over, and no sooner had I jarred to a halt when a car barrelled around the corner, just missing my wing mirror as he roared past. Taking a few deep breaths, I didn't need to look in the mirror to know my visiting guardian was gone. Message received. I feel that my life was saved that day, and every day I feel grateful that I understood to trust my energy and what I was seeing and hearing.

Your aura is created by the electrical and subtle energy fields powered from deep inside the electricity in every cell of your physical body. This energy emanates through your body, through your skin, and radiates all around you. Its massive job is to protect you, to connect you into yourself and all of creation, and it does this through vast and complex auric organisation borne out in layers and lemniscates. There is nothing random or coincidental about the intricate and complex patterns that it both creates and is created by. This is one of the beautiful aspects of your energy; it exists beyond duality in a place of continual unfolding and enfolding. It means that your energy system is always looking to find balance and harmony.

For a moment, just think about that. Your energy system is always looking to find balance and harmony. No matter what is going on with you right now, whether you are vibrant, resilient, and joyful or are struggling emotionally, physically, or with your life purpose, your own energy system is supporting you to find balance.

All of the lemniscates in your energy hold you lovingly, ready at all times to aid your balance, harmony, and health.

YOUR LUSCIOUS LEMNISCATE

One of the most exquisite of your energy patterns that support your balance and health is the *lemniscate*, or figure 8 pattern. I love the word lemniscate. From the Greek *lemniscatus*, it translates as 'decorated with ribbons,' and that is exactly what it looks like in your aura: billions of vibrant, pulsing ribbons that move and interact within a figure 8 pattern. Each lemniscate is coded with information carrying your template of health, and this template is connected through every single one of your energy systems and in every one of your cells. Lemniscate patterns are both huge (a single one embraces your entire body) *and* miniscule, with some being smaller than your DNA. They connect all that you are and hold you lovingly, ready at all times to aid your balance, harmony, and health.

There are so many case studies I could share with you about the power and efficacy of the aura in bringing profound transformation to people's lives. Some are complex and magnificent stories, yet the one that I want to share is simple and changed my life.

Jane came into my clinic after having experienced a heart attack. Her aura was so shrunken on her body that there were only a few tendrils pulsing out from her skin, and they were weak and looking for connection. The vast electrical organisation of her body and energy system was gone, and it looked like she was held together by the rigidity of shock alone. In her mid-60s, she had been enjoying a vibrant social life and seemingly good health up until her sudden heart attack, which was all the more shocking because she had thought she was in good health.

As she sat in the chair, Jane literally shook with exhaustion and deep despair at how her life had changed. What I was alarmed at was the lack of cohesion in any of the electrical currents in her body. It looked to me that if it wasn't for the medication she was taking, her heart wouldn't have been able to function in its physical form. I needed to be able to work in the most gentle and connective way, and in my mind, that meant immediately activating her lemniscates.

After explaining that I was going to be working exclusively with her aura and probably wouldn't touch her even once through the entire session (always a good thing to warn someone about!), I invited Jane to lie on the couch in whatever way she was most comfortable. She curled up on her side, and I covered her in blankets since she had been unable to get warm since her heart attack. Then I began.

One of the ways in which I see energy means that I can see the energy that *has been* present as well as the energy that *is* present. Every bit of your energy is coded in your energy fields, so by looking at the coding 'memory' of where Jane's aura had been before the heart attack, I could see that it had been vibrant, fun-loving, healthy, and big, enveloping her body by at least one to two metres. So that is where I started. Standing in that space nearly two metres from her physical body, I began to weave slow, gentle, horizontal 8s in her energy field, weaving her aura back into being and reminding it of its healthy programme. I knew it would take some time. For about 10 minutes, nothing happened, other than a slight sparking in her cells that were in line with the area I was working in. Gradually, those weak sparks of electrical connection began to pulse in more flow, even though it was still intermittent. This flow started to emanate out of Jane's physical body and create a small, weak auric field.

After 40 minutes of my supporting her lemniscates, Jane's aura was nearly a metre off her body and was beginning to weave tighter; if the aura were a tapestry, the picture wasn't very clear, but at least the fabric was there. After 60 minutes (and all this time I was simply weaving 8s in the space around her body), Jane was taking blankets off because she felt warm for the first time in four months. Her skin colour changed from grey to orangy-pink, and, most wonderfully to see, her eyes were twinkling. Her radiant life force was beginning to flow again. And still, I kept on working with her lemniscates.

By the time I stopped, after just over 90 minutes of weaving, Jane looked like a very different woman than the one who had walked into the clinic. It was as if life had reclaimed her once more. Her aura was filled with a golden energy that, over the years we worked together, I would get to know very well as her 'usual' colour that held all the other vibrations in her aura together. From that day on, she gradually regained her health, supporting herself by nurturing her luscious lemniscates at home. At first, she did so simply by doing exactly what I had been doing and tracing the 8 shape with her hands, but as she found increasingly more of her natural energy and zest for life returning, she discovered that music, and especially belly dancing, helped her aura more than anything else. She is still dancing to this day.

LAYER UPON LAYER OF WISDOM

In addition to lemniscates, you also have very specific layers or vibrational bands within your aura, each holding a certain level of information. Every layer is amazing and resonates with different vibrations within you, and because of this, they hold levels of coding about specific parts of your life and experiences. Your aura, as with all of your energy systems, is deeply in service to your becoming, and each layer helps inform and guide you in this process. Because of the coding running through every lemniscate, each layer of your aura connects deeply to all other layers, meaning that despite the distinct vibrations operating in every individual layer, your aura contains wholeness and wisdom response.

One of the most dynamic places in your whole body system is the place where your physical body ends and your exclusive energy body begins. When I look at the first layer of someone's aura, it is so close to their skin it looks like another layer of their physical body, or perhaps more like a reflection of their physical body, as if I am looking at it through a mirror. It is a fuzzy, staticky reflection, so think of looking through a dusty mirror (that takes no imagination in my household!). This interface is the very edge of your skin. If you can imagine a one millimetre space where your top-most layer of skin stops and the air around you begins, that is the first layer of your aura. It is bursting, packed, and exploding with your template of health and the consciousness of potential and is the powerful place where your physicality ends and meets the external. When you stroke your skin, you are also stroking that immense and powerful layer of the aura holding your template of health, and that in itself can help activate your energy system to support your physical and emotional health in every way.

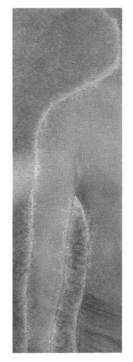

The energy in the first layer of your aura is buzzing with your template of health and the consciousness of potential.

One of the most dynamic places in your whole body system is the place where your physical body ends and your exclusive energy body begins.

THE POWER OF TOUCH

Do you doubt how powerful your auric interface and touch can be? Stroke your arm. How does it feel? Can you think of a time when someone stroked your skin with kindness? Or perhaps when you stroked a baby's face and saw them immediately relax? Studies show us the significant benefit of touch. This is partly because of the wonder of the skin, which is the second-largest organ in your body (second only to your large intestine, which has much more surface area than your entire skin). It is packed with millions of sensory receptors that gather all kinds of information, such as touch and temperature, and send it to the brain for processing, understanding, and appropriate reaction. The other reason touch has so many health and well-being benefits is because of what happens energetically as you stroke your skin; any time you touch your skin you are also activating this amazing interface layer, sending ripples through your entire body.

At the very edge of your aura is the final place of energetic interface. This is the auric membrane, where your unique and contained energy field meets everything else. It is at this final place where *you* energy interacts with and is, in part, defined by all *non-you* energy.

A few days ago, I was in a café (writing this book!), and sitting at a table close to me was a woman who was stressed and upset. Her energy was wired with a fight–flight–freeze programme, she was ungrounded, and noticeably locked in stress. Her friend reached across the table and took her hand, and the woman's system paused and moved towards groundedness. Then her friend stroked her arm as she was talking. It was as if the woman's fight–flight–freeze system simply became disabled; it dissolved before my eyes. She took a deep breath and closed her eyes for a moment. While that was happening, her energy systems began to move and flow again, and her natural radiance began to move from her core through her entire body and energy systems. That is what stroking the skin and the etheric layer of the aura can do and does – all the time.

WHAT DOES YOUR AURA DO?

Your aura is woven together like a beautiful and immense tapestry and has three main jobs, or at least, if we want to get all categorical about it, we can divide the thousands of jobs that your aura does into three main areas:

1. Protection.

2. Connection.

3. Communication.

Your physical, electrical, and subtle energy creates billions of filaments of energy (think billions of fine, pulsing, silver threads) that come from your body, move through your skin, and weave all around you to create your own magnificent and unique biofield. This tightly woven energy field acts as your first line of defence from *everything* that is outside of your own energy field.

Think of everything in terms of energy fields. Your friend is an energy field (a really lovely one). Your dog is an energy field (a deeply loyal one). Your garden and all the plants in it are energy fields. Everything in this web of life has its own energy field, and one of the crazy, yet wonderful aspects of understanding this is understanding where the meeting points of energy are.

If you are struggling with sustained stress, your aura can lock in patterns of defence and protection, keeping you in your habitual energy field and unable to experience balanced connection with yourself or others.

When you meet someone you are in conflict with, your aura/biofield can get all spiky and protective. You look like a hedgehog or porcupine with your bristles all sticking out. We even use this analogy in our language when we talk of someone being really bristly or 'bristling with anger.' Your aura shifts and changes continually, throwing itself open and expansive to some energies, people, and situations, and closing itself to others. If you are particularly sensitive to energy, you may notice that you feel closed and somehow tighter when you are in a big crowd. This is because your aura closes down and shrinks close to your body so that it can weave its billions of filaments super, super tightly to protect you from absorbing or merging with too much other energy. But what about when you are lying on the grass with your arms flung out, happy, relaxed, and delighted with your day? At that point, your aura is acting to connect you deeply with the magnificent energy of the land you are lying on, being supported, nourished, and revitalised.

Your aura is continually working to connect you to the supportive, nourishing, and perfect energy around you that is there for your continued growth and evolution along your life path. Your aura can wrap a friend in a perfect hug, connect into a vast forest of trees, or reach up to the stars to be blessed by the returning energy from the Cosmos.

Remember, you are never alone. You are always connected to this great cosmic web of life, and your aura is one of your most powerful connection points as you experience your unique and precious journey.

Take a moment to think about those vibrant pulsing silver filaments that are moving from your body, through your skin, and interweaving all around you. What are they pulsing with? Energy? Yes. But what is energy? The energy that moves through those filaments is the energy of life – *your* life – rich with your own life force and with the sentience and consciousness of you. 'You' are not just your brain, just your heart, or just your soul (not that there should be a 'just' before any of those nouns!). You are an interwoven field of wisdom, knowledge, curiosity, and wonder, and every part of you belongs in your essential place in this universe.

Because each auric filament holds this level of energy, each becomes an essential part of your energetic communication. That is why when you walk down a street and 'just' get a feeling that someone is watching you, you are right. Your energy field is not only communicating with the energy field of the person looking at you, but is also communicating this energy right back to you, to the part of you that only speaks the language of energy. The more you connect with this part of your awareness and don't dismiss it, the more you connect the bridge between this energetic communication and the sense-making part of your processing!

PRACTICES

Thinking:
Thinking Your Aura Magnificent

Your energy follows your thoughts, which makes you crazy powerful when it comes to influencing your energy (positively or not!). Think about what you have read here and perhaps already know about your aura, this amazing energy that emanates from deep inside of you and radiates through your skin, filling the space with tightly woven silver filaments of energy at least an arm's length from your body. Think about it; maybe visualise it. Look around you in this space and bring your awareness to what is there, even if you can't see it.

Feeling:
Powering Up the Auric Membrane

Breathe in, filling your lungs and your belly. As you breathe out, imagine the energy of your breath leaving through every pore of your skin, moving through the entire space of your aura until it gets to the amazing auric membrane. This 'skin' of your aura will receive this energy and use it to fuel the protection, connection, and communication of your entire auric system.

Doing:
Dance Your Aura to Feel Good!

Put on some music you love. The vibration of the music will begin to weave and dance with your auric filaments, enlivening your entire auric field. Dance, wobble, shake, move! There is nothing that your aura loves more than fun, dynamic movement.

The soul, like the moon,

is new and always new again.

~Lal Ded

(14th Century)

WE WOULD LOVE TO SUPPORT YOUR RADIANT SOUL JOURNEY

Get the most out of this book with;

- Video Guides – Let Prune guide you through the practices in this book.

- 3 Months Free Membership – Join our online community at The Gathering Ground where you can share, connect, and be inspired.

- Do you want to know your soul colour? – As a gift, we would like to give you Prune's book '*What is the colour of your soul?*'

Visit www.pruneharris.com/radiant-soul or scan the QR code

THE ELEMENTAL
RHYTHMS

*The ancients knew something
which we seem to have forgotten.
All means prove but a blunt
instrument, if they have not
behind them a living spirit.*

~Albert Einstein

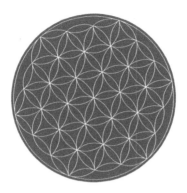

love the *elemental rhythms*! They are the energetic rhythm or vibration of life on Earth, and you are hardwired with them throughout every part of your energy, every part of your body, every part of you. In this chapter, we get to explore them, but, having taught about the *elemental rhythms* to thousands of students, I want to emphasise something right at the start of this chapter: The *elemental rhythms* are not a profiling system. They are not a psychological or character assessment tool, and they are not a way of popping yourself or others into a neat box of understanding, explaining, or justifying how you are. The *elemental rhythms* are vibrations that pulse rhythmically through your energy anatomy. They determine how your unique and amazing energy system vibrates, and therefore a lot of how you will perceive and interact with your world. When you understand the *elemental rhythms* and how they move through you, you can deeply understand, nurture, and balance them in yourself and live in your fullness.

Being aware of your elemental rhythms helps you make sense of how you are. They help explain why one person loves to party all night, while another prefers to curl up with a book and get an early night's sleep, or why one person can easily express their needs, while another spends most of their life learning how to. The elemental rhythms are amazing, astounding, and fascinating, and I am excited to share them with you here. (I will have to curb my enthusiasm through this chapter or you will get bored with the superlatives!)

One of the beautiful aspects of the energetic core is the way it is the interface between us as human beings and us as a part of something much, much bigger: the web of life that holds each of us strong, safe, and nourished on this amazing planet we call home.

You exist as a physical, emotional, and sacred human being *because* you are alive on Earth right now. This means that within your human energy fields is a constant presence of the qualities and aspects that are so familiar here on our planet: fire, air, water, and earth. Your physicality is imbued with the vibrations of these earthly elements, which have been recognised, written about, and used in medical clinical practices for thousands of years. And your energy system looks totally different depending on the balance of elemental rhythms that you hold.

As recently as 2,400 years ago, the Greek physician Hippocrates wrote about the four elements – water, fire, earth, and air – and their associated humours. Two thousand years before him, the ancient Indians combined their intricate and complex elemental understandings of space, air, water, earth, and fire to identify three body types, or *doshas*, known as *kapha*, *pitta*, and *vata*. At about the same time, the ancient Chinese were writing about health, life, and the Cosmos in relation to the five elements of water, wood, fire, earth, and metal.

The human energy system brings in the elements necessary for life on Earth through the *Sun star* and the *Earth star*, and these elemental aspects of your human energy system live balanced, intact, and whole deep within your energetic core.

Remember how I said that the energetic core is (sort of) like a hosepipe or a pole, with all its exquisite energy zooming through in radiant filaments, sending energy simultaneously from below your feet to above your head, and from above your head to below your feet? Well, at some point, this energetic pole meets the rest of your energy body as well as your physical body, and at this sacred interface something profound and magical happens. This interface point, running through the length of your body, is like a nuclear fusion of two energies combining together to create vast amounts of energy – energy that fuels your entire body and being. At this point of fabulous fusion, two amazing aspects of your energy field are created:

1. When all these filaments of coding that are running through your energetic core meet the rest of your energy field, it creates your unique template of health. This template of health holds the energetic coding for your fullness, your radiance, and your total physical, energetic, and sacred health. We will be exploring more about your template of health in a future chapter.

2. At this same point of fabulous fusion, the *elemental rhythms* that exist within your core coalesce into a specific and unique mix that will move through your whole body system. The equality of the *elemental rhythms* in your core shift and align so that the makeup of your unique, *elemental rhythm* and vibration will depend on what ratio of elements are being expressed within your specific energy system. Thus, you may have a predominance of the fire rhythm pulsing through your energy system, while a friend may have a predominance of the water rhythm pulsing through their whole body system.

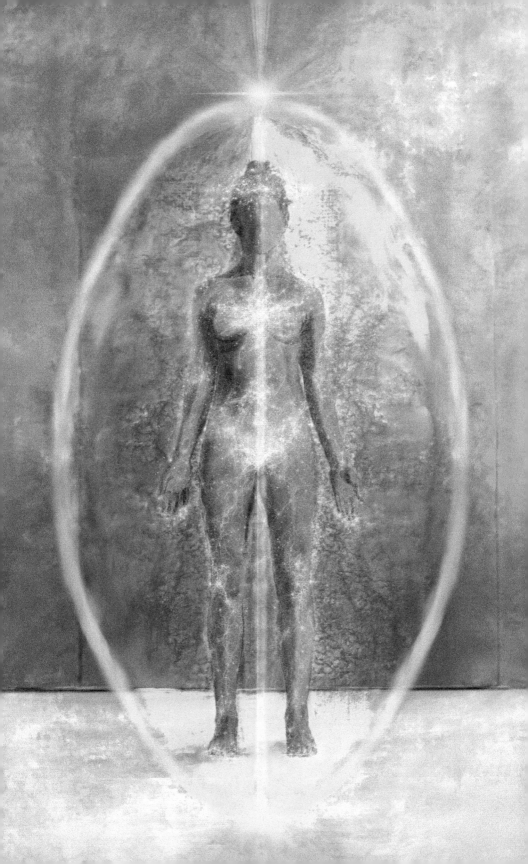

THE ELEMENTAL RHYTHM OF WATER

People who have more of the water rhythm emanating from their core are often big thinkers or philosophers of life. They may not move or speak very quickly, but what they have to say is always worth listening to. Waters take their time to do things and may not be too bothered about finishing projects. Their gift is to dream of a better world for all of us.

The energetic rhythm of water is lyrical, swaying, changing, and fluid, like a wave in motion. The energy flows from the core thickly and densely, feeding the cells, but it begins to dissipate rapidly in the aura. Sometimes, in people with a dominant water rhythm, this energy doesn't even make it to the skin very well. Water people can have significant challenges with their auric membrane because their energy can flow and merge so much.

- Shape/Direction: flowing fluidly up and down the body system.

- Related organs: kidney (yin) and bladder (yang).

- Related physiological systems: skeletal and excretory.

- In-balance emotions and attributes: bravery, determination, playfulness, innocence, wonder, enthusiasm, delight.

- Out-of-balance emotions and experiencing: fear, despair, futility.

The flowing and deep energy of water.

- Associated season: winter.

- Associated direction: north.

- Colour: black or deep blue.

THE ELEMENTAL RHYTHM OF FIRE

We are already quite familiar with people we may think of as 'fiery.' They are often very dynamic, fun people who laugh a lot and can really inspire us to be happy. They may also tire us out with their continued enthusiasm and unbridled spontaneity! They can sometimes be flighty and ungrounded and can be challenged by our social norm of going to bed at a 'reasonable time' and then getting up in the morning. Fire rhythm people like to party at night and sleep in!

The shape of fire is constantly changing, with much more fire in the top of the energy system than the bottom (from the waist up to above the head). It is a hot energy that can either scorch or envelop with warmth.

- Shape/Direction: moving up quickly and brightly; can have sudden bursts of passion and dynamism.

- Related organs: heart, small intestine, tongue.

- Related physiological system: circulatory.

The fast and dynamic energy of fire.

- In-balance emotions and attributes: joy, love, compassion, speaking the wisdom of the heart.

- Out-of-balance emotions and experiencing: panic, hysteria, bitterness, jealousy, hatred.

- Associated season: summer.

- Associated direction: south.

- Colour: red.

THE ELEMENTAL RHYTHM OF EARTH

People who have the earth rhythm emanating most strongly from their core are the carers of the world. They encircle others in their kindness and compassion and can often be found working as educators, for charities, or in healthcare professions. They have to be careful not to smother those they love and often need to learn the ability of looking after themselves as much as they look after others. They have a natural understanding of the rhythms of the natural world, being tuned into the diurnal rhythms of day and night and the rhythms of the seasons. A walk in nature is often the ideal medicine for earth rhythm people.

The shape of earth energy is round, and its sound is that of drumming, like the heartbeat of the Earth that moves through earth energy. It is a deep pulsing that moves out in waves from the core.

The kind and embracive energy of earth.

- Shape/Direction: spherical, embracive.

- Related organs: spleen and stomach.

- Related physiological system: digestive.

- In-balance emotions and attributes: stable, caring, compassionate, connected, gut wisdom, strong instinctive knowing, trust.

- Out-of-balance emotions and experiencing: resentment, feeling of inadequacy, need to be helpful, poking around in other people's business, overwhelm, dramatic despair, anxiety.

- Associated season: change of seasons (every third month relating to solstices and equinoxes).

- Associated direction: centre.

- Colour: yellow.

THE ELEMENTAL RHYTHM OF AIR/METAL

The first thing you might notice with this elemental rhythm is that, unlike the other elements, I am using two words to describe it. That is because I am trained in both ancient Celtic and ancient Chinese energetic understandings, and the ancient Chinese refer to this rhythm as metal. People who have the

The contained and inspirational energy of air/metal.

air/metal rhythm as the primary pulse of their core tend to be distinctive in their intellectual clarity and precision. These are the people who, in their balance, understand the cycle of life and death and look to transmute any experience into a deeper and spiritual understanding. As much as they can inspire, they can also be critical if they feel other people aren't doing something the way it 'should' be done.

The shape of the air/metal energy system is long, thin, and very dry. Its energy is held very tightly within the energetic core, often only just making it into the aura. There is nothing really exuberant about an air/metal energy system. It is controlled and precise.

- Shape/Direction: tall, thin, internal.

- Related organs: lung, large intestine, skin.

- Related physiological system: respiratory.

- In-balance emotions and attributes: feeling inspired, being inspiring, cosmic connection, wise acceptance.

- Out-of-balance emotions and experiencing: rigid, controlling, inability to let go or go with the flow, grief, judgement, regret.

- Associated season: autumn.

- Associated direction: west.

- Colour: white.

COMPLETING THE PUZZLE

The elemental rhythms are a huge passion of mine (have I said that already?), and along the pathway of my own learning, they stand out for me as an example of not being able to perceive something when you don't know it exists. I was always able to identify that there is an elemental rhythm that pulses from the core throughout the whole body system. I could watch how those rhythms coalesced in a specific layer of the aura, sharing information housed in that elemental vibration throughout the auric web and ensuring that its coding was present throughout every part of the whole body system. The life force in everyone is unique and depends on each person's particular blend/ratio of the rhythms, yet I still had an uneasy question somewhere deep in my awareness.

When I was at university and living with friends, one of my housemates always slammed doors. It wasn't that he was angry or dramatic, it was simply that every time he walked through a door, he shut it hard. He was, and still is, passionate about life, determined to live his life wholly, and committed to showing up fully for whatever experience he is presented with. He is dynamic and determined, and he moves through his life as a strong force of good. But I couldn't quite explain his rhythm. Deeply rooted in himself and his friendships, as well as in his loyalty, passion for life, and desire for justice, he had a strong pulse of the earth rhythm. Yet people with earth energy as their predominant rhythm have a spherical shape to their energy field, and he didn't. His was direct, strong, straight up, and straight down and was moving strongly forward from his body's energy field. It wasn't the rhythm of fire, it wasn't the rhythm of water, and it wasn't the rhythm of air or air/metal, so if I thought about it, I had to house his energy system in the rhythm of earth. But I knew it wasn't quite right.

Then, in my training in Touch for Health kinesiology, I was introduced to the ancient Chinese understanding of the elemental rhythms and had to redefine everything I understood about them! Instead of identifying four elements in the Cosmos (and therefore, the human energy system), they identify five: water, wood, fire, earth, and air/metal.

The air/metal element was very familiar, as it was simply a different way of describing what I had been identifying as air in my previous understanding. But *wood*? What kind of elemental rhythm was that? The more I read about and studied the five elemental rhythms, the more I fell in love with the dual nature and immense simplicity, subtlety, and complexity of Chinese understandings. I invited myself to look for this mysterious 'wood' rhythm with its dynamic and determined energy. The more I looked, the easier it was to identify, and soon, I had shifted my perception to incorporating this awareness in every aspect of my understanding of energy. But I had to know what I was looking for, so I needed to be introduced to it before I could perceive it. My hope is that the understanding in this book will do exactly the same for you, introducing you to the simple wonder of your energy systems so you can become increasingly more empowered to perceive them and help balance them towards their natural health and vitality.

THE ELEMENTAL RHYTHM OF WOOD

People who primarily have a wood rhythm at their core often move very quickly indeed. They stride as they walk, they can talk and think fast, and they can get impatient or even angry when others can't keep up. They are the movers and doers of our world. They can take the ideas that water rhythms present and turn them into reality.

The shape of wood energy is solid and thick, with energy coming off the core and into the exterior. Wood energy vibrates a lot, as it is a very strong energy and a highly charged battery. Out-of-balance wood looks like numerous lightning bolts coming from the solar plexus, and it can be destructive.

- Shape/Direction: forward moving, external.

- Related organs: liver and gallbladder.

- Related physiological system: all self-regulatory systems in the body.

- In-balance emotions and attributes: expansiveness, compassion, assertion, profound sense of justice.

- Out-of-balance emotions and experiencing: anger, impatience, frustration, irritation.

- Associated season: spring.

———————————————→

The strong and determined energy of wood.

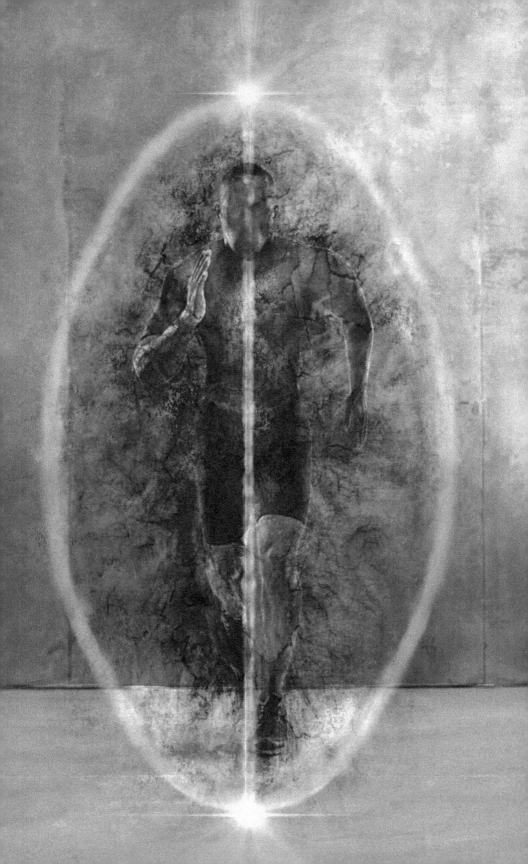

- Associated direction: east.

- Colour: green.

THE FIVE ELEMENTAL RHYTHMS AND YOU

At any point in your life, you always house all elemental rhythms in your energetic core and therefore through your energy fields, yet the fundamental balance of them will be specific to you. It may be useful for you to think about the relationship of the elemental rhythms in terms of percentage. Constitutionally, your friend may be 45 percent fire, 25 percent earth, 15 percent water, 10 percent air/metal, and five percent wood, while you may be 30 percent wood, 30 percent earth, 20 percent air/metal, 10 percent fire, and 10 percent water . . . and so on.

This is why sometimes you can be so similar to someone else, and sometimes you can be poles apart. If you and your brother have a very similar ratio of elemental rhythms, for example, then there will be a lot of similarities; if your ratios are very different, then there will be great differences. And this isn't just experienced in your energy fields. Remember that your energy fields determine and affect everything about your physicality, your emotions, and your character, and this is *especially* true of the way your elemental rhythms affect you.

One of the most powerful ways you can engage in your own healing and becoming is by bringing balance to your elemental rhythms. The elemental rhythms are fascinating enough in their complexity that I know I could study them my entire life and still have much to learn. Yet they also hold such stark and simple truths that even grasping the basic understandings brings deep changes into your daily life. Let me give you a more everyday example of how they are useful.

When my son and daughter were 12 and nine, respectively, I was browsing through the paper one day and saw that a boy band was playing in our local concert venue that night. I called my daughter, who was playing at a friend's house, and asked her if she would like to go if I could get tickets. She said she would *love* to, so I got the tickets and let her know I would pick her up in 20 minutes. I was excited to be sharing this first concert with her!

When my daughter got into the car, she burst into tears. Sobs and words poured out of her because she didn't know what she should do. She was supposed to be having a sleepover with her cousin that night, she had been invited to play with another friend, and now there was a concert. She didn't want to let anyone down. She was (hiccup) just (sob) so (sob, sob, sob) upset (wail). I was flabbergasted and a bit annoyed. Here I was organising this lovely and exciting thing for us to do, and she was breaking down in overwhelm and hysterics. But I knew the rhythms and knew that in this situation, her loving and loyal earth rhythm was feeling totally overwhelmed at the thought of letting friends down. At the same time, her fire rhythm had hit the panic button, ungrounding her and shooting her straight towards hysteria. From this place, she was now in emotional and energetic freefall, unable to access logical thought or a place of stability to think this through.

'Come on,' I said, 'let's go and get a drink and figure it out.' Earths love food and drink; it can be deeply grounding and help bring back stability.

We walked into the kitchen, where my son, Rowan, looked up at his sister, very surprised by the state she was in, and asked what was wrong. Between her sobs and upset, she told him.

He put his arms around her and said, 'But Ella, it's OK. Go to the concert tonight, because it's only here for one night. Play with your friend tomorrow day, and have a sleepover with your cousin tomorrow night. That all works fine, doesn't it?'

As my son radiated his strong wood and air/metal elemental vibrations with their deep sense of safety, logic, and strength, Ella looked at him and stopped crying immediately.

'Yes,' she said, 'that's OK.' And with that, her earth rhythm processed and stabilised, integrating the shifting possibility of being able to meet all needs, including her own.

'So you'll go to the concert tonight?' he asked.

'Yes.'

'So go get ready!'

'OK!' she said, and her fire grounded down, sparking into joy.

Now that it was clear how to manage her loyalty to her friends and the excited overwhelm that had come into her system, she ran up the stairs, already happy and looking forward to the night. Fires love a party, and her fire was now expanding into joy and excitement. (And we had a *great* night!)

SOUNDS FUN, BUT WHY IS IT IMPORTANT?

Just as you would readily say that the fire burning in your woodstove has a very different quality and vibration than the water in your cup, so people with greater quantities of the *elemental rhythm* of fire in their system have very different qualities and vibration than those with greater quantities of the *elemental rhythm* of water in their system. Because the vibrational pulse moves from your core through your whole body system, including your aura and your auric membrane, you literally vibrate with the elemental balance that was created at that interface, or fabulous fusion point. And depending on your specific mix of *elemental rhythms*, your energy system will move in a very specific direction and hold a very specific shape. This vibration will also move through all of your organs, and the organs in your body that resonate more with that specific mix will take their place slightly more strongly in your energetic and physical makeup than those that don't. Your *elemental rhythm* mix determines your natural emotional responses, and the way people perceive you will depend on the makeup of your *elemental rhythms*. A lot of the words your friends would use to describe you provide a powerful insight into which of the rhythms pulse most strongly in your system.

Understanding your *elemental rhythms* helps you do all the following:

- Understand yourself and others.

- Bring more compassion to yourself and others.

- Make sense of why you naturally gravitate towards certain things, people, and ways of being.

- Feel like you belong (in your own body, in your own family, in your world).

- Know how to deeply nurture yourself.

- Stop comparing yourself negatively to other people.

- Perceive and understand your strengths and challenges more easily.

- Have understandings, techniques, and insights into how to bring yourself deeper and deeper into balance, harmony, and joy.

You are an amazing and unique blend of all of these elemental rhythms of life.

One of the most important things to understand about the *elemental rhythms* is that each rhythm holds the full spectrum of balance and imbalance. Right now, the fire vibration in your body may be in beautiful health, harmony, and balance, or it may be crashing around, throwing off your potential for stability, happiness, and joy in your daily life. Your Earth *elemental rhythm* may be holding you strong, compassionate, and deeply content, or it may be out of balance. If it is the latter, it may mean that you are spending so much time giving to other people that you are neglecting your own needs, sending you crashing back into resentment, misery, and a sense of being totally on your own.

Jamie and Emma brought their son, Henry, into my clinic when he was three months old and covered with eczema. They had been working with specialist dieticians and dermatologists, but nothing was improving it. As I looked at his energy system, there was one very striking imbalance, and it was in his air/metal *elemental rhythm*. Physiologically, the vibration of air/metal governs the lungs, the large intestine, the skin, and the hair, so it made sense that the air/metal being out of balance in his system could be affecting his skin.

But why would a baby have such a strong imbalance in his air/metal rhythm?

When a baby is born, its specific ratio of elemental rhythms is already well established. Often, it is even very visible while still in the womb, as the elemental vibration of the baby emanates well into the mother's aura. For nine months, the baby grows inside not only the mum's physical body, but also her energy fields. And when that baby is born, the connection between the mum and baby's energy fields continues. It is a gradual process, and one that takes about two years before the child's energy system is truly separate from the mum's energy field. And of course, as many mums know, there is a connection that lasts for life.

Little Henry was held deeply within his mum's energetic field. Their auras were interlinked, as is normal and healthy for every child, but Emma's air/metal rhythm was deeply, deeply strained, almost to breaking point. It was showing up as a rigid energy around her lungs and chest, a tight constriction around her heart, and a general rigidity through her entire system. I could see that Emma was continually wrestling with controlling her ability to function and that it was at an enormous cost. Air/metal has a close association with the emotion of grief, and I could see grief dripping through all of Emma's system.

I turned my attention to Emma and asked her how she was.

'Fine,' she said. 'We are here about Henry.'

It is a tricky conversation to start with a loving mum, telling her that it is her system that is affecting the health of her child. Yet, in my experience, truth shared compassionately is always healing.

I explained about the qualities of the energy of metal and how it is associated with grief, and I asked her whether she was experiencing any grief. Everything in her system tightened, almost to a point of stillness. I then explained how babies are held in their mother's energy fields and described how her energy field was showing up, asking if I could help her. As she broke down in tears, her overly tight metal system cracked, and her system became flooded with the healing balance of water. At last, she no longer had to hold things together so very, very tightly.

For several weeks, Emma and I worked in the clinic together as she mourned the loss of her first child, who had died before he was born. She had taken time between his death and getting pregnant with Henry, and had thought her grief and loss had completed and healed. But after Henry was born, her pain was present in every new development Henry went through, which was crippling her. Her strongest *elemental rhythms* were water and air/metal, with earth, fire, and wood all much weaker. The imbalance and pain in her air/metal element had thrown off all the natural balance in her system until it was holding everything taut, tight, and brittle. Water has a strong association with fear and courage, too, and the tightness in her air/

metal *elemental rhythm* meant she was experiencing increasing fear that she would never be able to move this crippling grief through her system. It was these elemental imbalances that were so affecting Henry's skin.

Bringing the balance back to Emma's *elemental rhythms* returned balance to her whole body system, and she was able to honour her love and grief for her first son while still delighting more and more in the life of her second. And, as she found healing within her, Henry's skin recovered, and his eczema melted away.

PRACTICES

 Thinking:
Exploring the Elements

By looking around you at the natural world, think about how you would describe the different qualities of the rhythms. If you were asked to talk about the different vibrations or energies of water, fire, earth, wood, and air/metal, what words would you use? I encourage you to not only think about how you would do it, but find the actual words. Speak aloud how you would describe the different qualities or vibrations of these elements to a friend, or write them down in a journal or notebook.

 Feeling:
Elemental Organs

Tune into your perceptions of the *elemental rhythms*. Bring to mind fire, water, wood, earth, and air/metal. Now, place your hands over your heart, feeling its beat. Take your awareness deeper, towards the organ itself. If you could identify which of the rhythms is most prevalent in your heart organ, which would it be? Take the time to tune into your heart and feel into each of the rhythms. Which one most seems to fit with your body? Your heart? Your being?

One at a time, do this same practice with your hands over your kidneys, your stomach, your liver, and your lungs. Do they feel elementally different or the same?

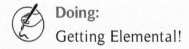

Doing:
Getting Elemental!

In order to more deeply understand how the *elemental rhythms* flow through your life, try to understand them more in their natural and magnificent environment:

- Water: Take time to sit in contemplative stillness next to your favourite body of water.

- Wood: Support a local woodland or forest through volunteering, tree planting, or helping raise funds. How does it feel to be helping the trees?

- Fire: Enjoy being around a fire with friends, whether inside or outside. Feel the warmth and vital necessity of friendship and community.

- Earth: Observe the change of the seasons from your window, and then get outside and *be part* of the changing seasons. Plant those tiny seeds, harvest your bounty, kick the piles of leaves, and let go of stuff that is no longer aiding your life. Rest deep in the cold of winter.

- Air/Metal: Feel the air on your skin. Notice how it changes daily, sometimes barely a whisper and other times a strong blow. When you are out in the wind, how does it affect the breath as it comes into your body? What air do you love breathing in? Cool? Warm? Humid? Get analytical and curious.

We have calcium in our bones, iron in our veins, carbon in our souls, and nitrogen in our brains. 93 percent stardust, with souls made of flames, we are all just stars that have people names.

~Nikita Gill
(1987–present)

THE ENERGY
CHANNELS
SYSTEM

Concerning matter, we have been all wrong. What we have called matter is energy, whose vibration has been so lowered as to be perceptible to the senses. There is no matter.

~Albert Einstein

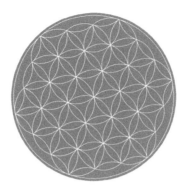

You may be familiar with the fact that there are channels that carry your blood to every part of your body. These are your capillaries, veins, and arteries. In exactly the same way, there are channels that carry energy to every part of your body. These channels are called meridians. You might not have learned about them in your school biology lessons, but these channels have been superbly documented by the Chinese, the Indians, and many other cultures for over five thousand years.

There are three distinct energy channel systems:

1. The *nadis*, or songlines.

2. The extraordinary channels.

3. The organ meridian system.

Each of them plays a different role in helping your energy move throughout every part of your whole body system.

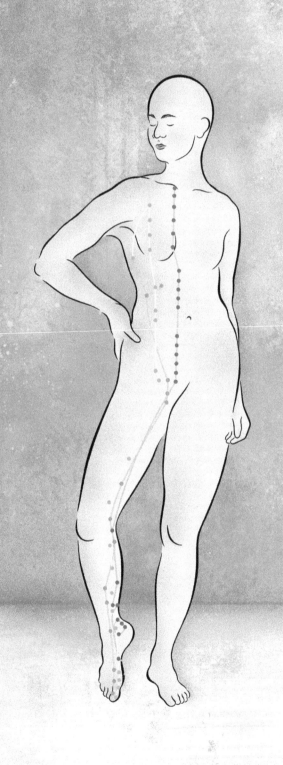

And just as your veins, capillaries, and arteries are integral to your physical system, these energy channels are integral to every single part of your energy anatomy.

You have already read about the aura. The *nadis* are key components of your aura. Think back to the chapter about the energetic core; the extraordinary channels come from the energetic core and are one of the biggest healing forces in your system. They carry consciousness, radiance, and healing through your system and beyond. You have also read about *elemental rhythms*. The organ meridian system carries your specific *elemental rhythms* through your body, picking up information from organs relating to each rhythm and sharing this information throughout.

And, just to add a bit more complexity, these three distinct channels often don't remain separate from each other and can hitch a ride on each other at times. So, if I were working clinically and wanted to help a client activate their *nadis*, the first place I would pay attention to is their extraordinary channels, for the extraordinary channels feed the energy that the *nadis* flow from. Think of a network of roads across a nation; there are tiny roads that connect villages, mid-sized roads that connect towns, and highways that connect cities. Within each city is the same division of tiny roads, medium roads, and highways. Depending on where you are going on your own journey, you

←————————————

You have multiple channels that carry energy and information through your whole body system.

may travel on all three of these types of roads, or only one. This is exactly the situation that happens in your energy channels. Each channel has a specific direction, route, and purpose, and, when in connective balance, will achieve this purpose in the most streamlined and efficient way with energy flowing from one channel to the next.

Let's take a look at what each of these energy systems holds in its unique vibration.

THE NADIS

I love the *nadis*! Just thinking about them gets my nadi system hum-hum-humming. Beginning deep in the lower abdomen, in an energy centre called your *lower dantian*, the *nadis* create an interconnected web of energy made up of vibrating, resonating filaments. They are an amazing part of your energy anatomy that sing your body into being, and because of this, I have always referred to them as the 'songlines' of the body.

The *nadis* run on the skin, under the skin, deep in the tissues, and wrap around the organs. They exist throughout all the aura, weave and connect into all the chakras, and connect with and to every part of you. In Ayurvedic health philosophy, it is understood that there are 101 main nadi channels in the body. Each of these 101 channels splits off to create a total of 72,000 in the whole-body field, with a dense concentration around your navel, your heart, and your brain, where you have three powerful energy centres called dantians.

The word *nadi* derives from the Sanskrit word *nad*, meaning 'hollow stalk, sound vibration, and resonance.' When I discovered this, I was delighted at the similarity in name between what I had perceived them to be and what they have been known for for thousands of years. That is one of the beautiful and fascinating things about energy: no matter what healing tradition, from what country, at whatever time in human history, the human energy system remains the same. There may be different names or variants around how it is interpreted, but the essence of human energy remains universal, reminding us that we are all the same, even in our beautiful uniqueness.

The *nadis* were one of the parts of energy anatomy that took me the longest to identify, as the vibration of this part of your energy is attuned to all other parts of the human energy

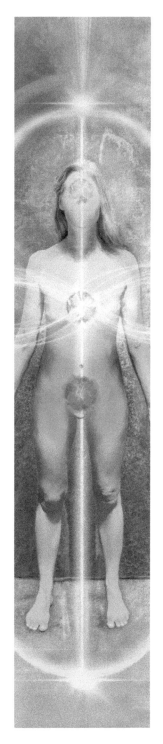

You have a dense concentration of nadis around your navel, your heart, and your brain, where you have three powerful energy centres called dantians.

system. It would be like me asking you to perceive the water in your physical body. You know that you are made of 70 percent water, yet it isn't like you could show me the water in your body. It is the same way with the songlines.

Songlines are everywhere, yet they are indistinct from other parts of your energy anatomy. I first really started noticing them when I would be working with a client and hear the songlines activate when deep healing was taking place, for they would begin to resonate, to hum, to sing in a different way.

It is this pulsing vibration that led me to give *nadis* the name 'songlines,' as that is what they seem to me. They sing the body alive, and when you connect with them, when you tune into them, you hear the vibration of your body. The more you connect to them, the more you hear the song of your body, the song of your spirit, the song of your soul.

THE EXTRAORDINARY CHANNELS

The extraordinary channels carry the light and wisdom of your *Radiant Soul* energy held within your energetic core. They radiate from the core, wrapping through and around you to ensure that your physical body can always be nurtured by this soul energy. One of my favourite teachers, scholar and Celtic Shaman Caitlin Matthews, once talked to me about how the body is 'marinated in the soul.' I would completely agree, and it is through these extraordinary channels that this marinating happens.

The key takeaway about the extraordinary channels is that they are deep, wide, and light-filled, which means they carry radiance wherever they flow. This energy can heal your physical body and support and balance your emotional and cognitive states. These channels also carry your profound connective energy, because they come from the energetic core that is nourished by planetary and cosmic energies and are beautifully and uniquely you. Think of a time when you have experienced beauty. Perhaps you have been deeply touched by a sunset, a painting in a gallery, or the wisdom in a child's smile. At that point, your extraordinary channels were in full flow. They were connecting the energy of your essence with the energy of the world's essence. I would even go as far as to say that your extraordinary channels connect your individual soul with the world's soul. When they are active, the energy of compassion, generosity, kindness, and deep wisdom will be flowing through every cell of your body and bringing that vibration out into the world around you.

As I think of the extraordinary channels, I think of the thousand stories I could share of seeing them activate in quite extraordinary ways. For when they activate, they can flood your system in ways that envelop everything you are, everything you think, and everything you feel. I want to share two stories here, both about the birth of my children.

Our first child, Rowan, was a big baby at nine pounds, nine ounces, and it took a while for my body to give birth to him. Both times I gave birth, I had planned home births, and both times, I ended up being in the hospital (a great lesson that any pre-existing plans about being a parent get crumpled up and

thrown out as soon as they are planned!). My husband, Collin, had been present and active during every step of Rowan's birth, and his extraordinary channels were just as present as he was. Partly, his extraordinary channels were so present because mine were. Every birthing woman, whether they are relaxed, joyous and empowered, or tense and scared, is within the sacred and immense energy of birth, and this means that their extraordinary channels are powerfully active. Because they are so deeply connective, when your extraordinary channels are active, they also nourish them in people around you. So Collin's extraordinary channels were already active, thick, big, and flowing through his system, but there was also tiredness, concern, uncertainty, and everything else that can be present for a father supporting the arrival of his child.

I can see it before my eyes now as clearly as when it was happening. The second Collin took his son in his arms, a profound readjustment occurred in his energy fields. His extraordinary channels surged and expanded so that his entire system lit up. They were flooding his *nadis* with radiant energy. This, in turn, lit up the system of our son, and there was recognition between them at the level of the soul, a connection into and a claiming of each other at an energetic level. It was an exchange and a moment that occurred before my eyes. It was real and profound, one that existed outside of time and space,

←———————

Your extraordinary channels carry your wild wisdom through the rest of your energy fields.

sharing a flash of coding and light information into the great cosmic web of life.

This is the immense potential of your extraordinary channels – to both receive information from this web of life and recode it to shape and evolve your conscious world a little differently.

The second story concerns the birth of our daughter, Ellarose. Seven months into my pregnancy, I became very ill with a virus. A high fever and extreme sensitivity to light and noise incapacitated me, and she was born several weeks early. As I was on my way to the hospital, I squeezed the hand of my midwife during a strong contraction. She looked me straight in the eye and said in no uncertain terms that I was too ill to make any excess effort like that. She told me my fever was so high that I would be unable to receive any medication or anaesthetic if the birth got complicated, so I was to go straight into the part of my body that allowed it and my baby to do the birth without any conscious thought or effort on my part. (Yes, she is an amazing midwife, and she had spent many years working in birthing houses in Asia.) And so I did. I felt all my consciousness settle into the deep pathways of my extraordinary channels and energetic core. I said nothing, heard nothing, and wanted no one to touch me. I felt in no way an interactive human; the only thing of which I was aware was the deep, slow throbbing of energy that was causing my own physicality to shift, change, and open.

I was also aware of another energy: the energy of the baby. I could see her energy light up stronger and stronger. My own physical energy was very poor, as I was depleted after three weeks of illness, yet here was this little physical powerhouse moving her way through my body, being an active part of her own birth, of her own coming into the world. Her extraordinary channels were, and still are, extra-extraordinary! As she entered the world and the room, there was a moment when her channels shifted from their single focus of direction (birth) to a radiant expression of life. Think of a light wave suddenly expanding. From her centre, it vibrated through the whole room and then settled back a little closer to her body field. As she left my protective energy field, no longer housed exclusively in my own electromagnetic energy, her own energy field met the energy of the planet and the energy of the Earth, and the meeting lit her up.

Ella's sense of belonging has been immense since that time, even to the extent that when she was four years old and sitting beside us in bed one day with colouring pens and a notebook, she asked me to help her spell out some words.

'I've written "I,"' she said. 'How do I spell "am?"'

'A. M.,' I answered.

'How do I spell "myself?"'

'M. Y. S. E. L. F.'

'"Being?"'

'B. E. I. N. G.'

'"Loved?"'

'L. O. V. E. D.'

I looked at what she had written and then decorated with coloured pictures of flowers growing from the Earth: 'I am myself, being loved.' That is extraordinary channel wisdom, power, and awareness.

THE ORGAN MERIDIAN SYSTEM

Energy operates in your body at different levels and different vibrations. Some, like the extraordinary channels, are vast and expansive, while others are more focused and contained, and this is the case with the organ meridian system. Based on ancient Chinese wisdom, the organ meridian system has been catalogued for thousands of years, even showing up as tattoos

Your extraordinary channels are deep, wide, and light-filled, which means they carry radiance wherever they flow.

on a five-thousand-year-old mummified body in the Otz valley between Austria and Italy.[1]

Each of your organs has an energy channel associated with it to help maintain flow and balance throughout your vital physical functions. If there was just one word that I would use to describe the organ meridian system most accurately, it is 'relational.' Every single section, action, understanding, sentience, wisdom, and function within the organ meridian system is in service to the whole. Your organ meridian system understands the details of keeping energy flowing through your body so that your physicality can be nourished, healthy, and vital. Thank you, organ meridian system!

Although these organ channels are categorised into 12 different meridians, they form one immense and seamless network of connected energy lines, all involved in helping maintain your health. There is beautiful symmetry in your organ meridian system, with different partnerships and relationships ensuring the system remains connective and balanced. Every yin meridian has a partner yang meridian that it can borrow energy from or give energy to. In relation to the elemental rhythms, the meridians hold a different relationship, with groupings of two or four meridians helping to bring checks and balances into your physical, emotional, and connective energy bodies. Each of your meridians has set pathways and is responsible for specific tasks within your body system.

---

[1] Leopold Dorfer et al., "A Medical Report from the Stone Age?" *The Lancet* 354, no. 9183 (September 18, 1999): 1023–1025, https://doi.org/10.1016/S0140-6736(98)12242-0.

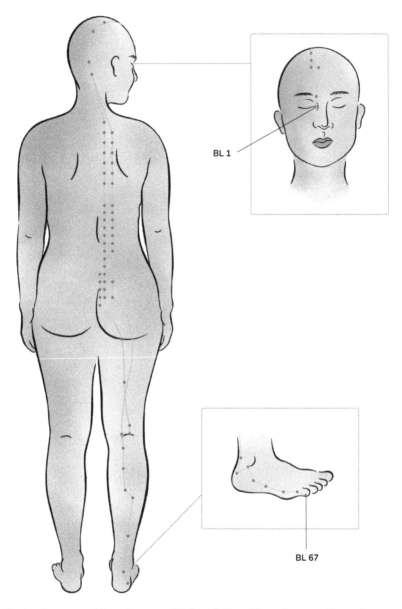

BL 1

BL 67

Each of your meridians have multiple relationships of energetic exchange. This image shows the pathway of the Bladder Meridian with the multiple points on it where such energetic exchange can be affected and enhanced.

The most superficial aspect of the organ meridian system runs just under your skin, forming the outer network of flow. Other sections of your organ meridian system travel deeper into your body, sometimes through your organs, sometimes wrapping around them, and other times, diving deep into your body to connect to other energy systems such as the extraordinary channels, the bone marrow, and the brain.

The organ meridians are the workers of your energy system, continually doing their job of maintaining flow and balance. They are a stalwart of any energy practices or clinical work that you may do to aid your health and vitality. It is into acupoints along the meridians that acupuncturists place their needles or use acupressure to enhance flow, connectivity, and balance.

In my clinical practice, I would hold the meridians in awareness in every session, even if I did not work directly on them. I would look elsewhere in the energy systems for whatever work we were doing to connect, nourish, or clear congestion in each of the 14 meridians in the client's body, for then I knew the balance would be brought deeply into the physical body.

When Ed first arrived at the clinic, he was in constant pain in every joint, every muscle, and seemingly every organ. Each breath caused pain, and as he breathed in and out, a tense ripple of shock moved through his weak and tiny aura.

Ed had a rare genetic condition called Ehlers-Danlos syndrome and had lived with pain, weakness, and all the grave limitations brought by the symptoms of the syndrome since he was a teenager. He did not expect anything we did to help, as he had tried several other treatment modalities, but he was determined for his own sake and the sake of his loving partner to try any option available.

When there is constant and chronic pain in the body, the energy channels get very quiet. The constant humming, buzzing, and general workability of the channels dims, as though all systems are creeping on eggshells, trying to function at the lowest cost to the overall energy system. People who live in pain have some of the quietest systems I ever see. Instead of the continual roll of expansion and contraction occurring throughout the field, everything is taut, tight, and restricted. It isn't quite that everything has the vibration of the habitual field through it, however, for there can be great consciousness and connectedness in people who experience the deep initiatory process of experiencing the limitation of chronic pain.

Ed was no exception to this pattern of energetic restriction and tattered aura, nor to the soul wisdom borne through initiation, for his heartfield and his energetic core beat a rhythm of determination and willing connection. There was a joy and lightness in his energetic rhythms, with humour running through them, yet he wasn't able to carry that through into his daily life because of the effect that constant pain was having on him.

What was most noticeable in Ed's system was that his meridian channels were far less vibrant than they were designed to be. Energy eked through them, meagre and low functioning. I felt there were two main clinical choices. One was to work to help his deep energy flow through the rest of his energy systems by activating more of the radiance of his energetic core; this would help it flow through his extraordinary channels and into his organ meridian system so it could affect his physical body on every level. The other was to nurture and connect his organ meridian system so that it could receive more of Ed's essential energy. The primary mandate of anyone who works with health care, whether they are trained in biomedical or holistic health, is 'primum non nocere,' or 'first, do no harm.' At this point of choice, I suspected that increasing the vigour of flow from Ed's energetic core may create a pushing of energetic movement and be too much for his system to handle, so I chose to focus on his organ meridian system.

We began by smoothing out his meridian system, using my hands to trace each meridian in the direction of flow that was healthy and connective. Because these channels exist just under the skin, they respond immediately to the electromagnetic energy that continually emits from the hand. As we worked, I was always watching for any push back or reactiveness from the meridian system, but there was none, just a deep willingness on the part of the organ meridian system to accept the increase in energy. Little by little, points in Ed's body began filling with more energy and lighting up in the process.

Along every organ meridian are powerful points that store energy to manage the overall flow throughout the meridian system. They are known as 'yuan' or 'source' points, both for the way in which they are connected to deeper source energy within you and for the way in which they source energy throughout your body system. They have a special relationship with the physical organs that you house and, when there is a need, will direct energy from their own little reservoirs and shoot it along the meridian system directly into the related organ. This is what began to happen in Ed's system.

I watched each source point progressively go from looking like a dried-up bog to more of a tiny lake or reservoir, connected to far deeper energy. As Ed's exquisite core energy was able to flow into his extraordinary channels more, they in turn sourced the source points, which in turn increased their flow to the organs along his organ meridian system. Have you ever watched a sped-up film of a motorway intersection flyover as dusk moves towards night and all the cars turn their lights on? Suddenly, where there had been cars, roads, and surroundings, there are now bright lights seemingly making an unbroken stream along the highway. Well, this is what Ed's system looked like! Streaks of energy moving throughout. And he could breathe without pain. He could move without pain. He looked 20 years younger as we sat to go through the ways he could continue to support his meridian system while at home. Tracing, connecting, sourcing meridians, and helping them maintain their flow have become normal and natural practices for Ed. He continues to live with Ehlers-Danlos syndrome, but he is able to engage in his life much more fully and joyfully.

PRACTICES

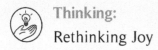 **Thinking:**
Rethinking Joy

One of the easiest ways to activate your extraordinary channels is to connect to the joy that already exists in your day. It is an energetic fact that like attracts like, so when you notice joy, you create joy, which in turn helps you notice joy, which helps you create joy (you get the picture!).

Think back along your day, or if you are reading this first thing in the morning, then think back along your day yesterday. If you are actively looking for something joyous along this timeline, what pops out for you in your awareness? You might not have experienced joy at the time, because you may not have noticed it as worthy of joy, but that is one of the benefits of energetic hindsight! Perhaps there was a lovely cloud formation in the sky that now, with intention and time, you can identify as beautiful or amazing. Perhaps a family member did something kind for you that you thanked them for, but now you identify the joy that that kindness offered you. Perhaps you remember a child laughing or being determined about something, and now, as you think about it, you feel glad for them; you feel joy. Go through your day and bring this awareness forward. Not only will you benefit from the increased activation of your extraordinary channels, but you will also be priming your energy fields to identify the small and profound places in your daily life that bring you joy in all its healing forms.

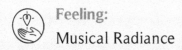

Feeling:
Musical Radiance

For this practice, you need a way to listen to your favourite music. Before you turn your music on, get comfortable and tune into how you are feeling. Check in with how you feel physically and emotionally and how connected you feel to the world around you. Now, turn on your music at a volume that you love. Allow the music to wash over you for several minutes and then check in again with how you feel physically, emotionally, and connectively.

Doing:
Enhance Your Flow, Balance Your Energy

This simple and powerful practice activates your organ meridian system in the direction that the system flows in balance and health. You can do this every day to enhance your vitality and whole-body wellness.

1. Place both hands on your chest and take a grounding breath in and out, connecting with the energy of your heart.

2. Circle your hands over your chest, activating the energy around your heart.

3. From this central place, use your left hand to stroke all the way down the inside of your right arm, through your palm, and off your fingertips. Now do the same with your right hand, stroking all the way down the inside of your left arm.

4. Place your left hand on the back of your right hand and stroke all the way up the top side of your arm, through your neck, and up to your face. Do the same on the opposite side by using your right hand to stroke the back of your left hand, the top side of your left arm, and all the way to your face.

5. With both palms on your face, stroke them up over your hairline, over your head, and all the way down your back, glutes, back of your legs, and off your heels.

6. Place both hands over the tops of your feet, with your fingers covering the top of your toes. Now stroke to your ankles and up the inside of your leg, continuing to stroke up your body until you arrive back at your chest.

7. Once more, circle your hands over your chest, rubbing your skin to activate your heart's energy.

8. Cross your hands over your heart and take another nourishing breath.

Remember, I have created videos of many of the practices in this book, so I can guide you as we do them together. You can find these videos and other supporting material at www.pruneharris.com/radiant-soul.

It is never too late to be

what you might have been.

~George Eliot

(1819–1880)

THE CHAKRAS

Everything that exists in your life, does so because of two things: something you did or something you didn't do.

~Albert Einstein

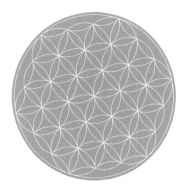

Your chakras are one of the wonders of your energy anatomy. I am in awe of them and their immensity. One of the reasons for this deep love is that chakras are deeply connected to our physical bodies. Think of them not as something that exists in your energy field or that you live within, but rather as a system that your own physical body creates, with the exception of the deep seed of cosmic coding that exists at the centre of every chakra. Chakras are amazing, dynamic, sneaky, protective, blazing, roaring, slamming, grabbing, poking, demanding, generous . . . and awesome!

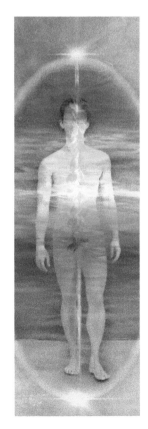

Because chakras are one of the most complex of all energy systems, it could take several books to explain all their intricacies, so forgive me for my choices in what I share in this overview and what I omit. It is my intention in this chapter to inspire you to love your chakra system and get curious to know more.

A GRADUAL UNDERSTANDING

I was very much a latecomer to the chakra system. I have always been able to see it, but somehow it just didn't grab me with interest. I couldn't find a natural resonance with it. When I look at and explore the electrical system of the body, I get uber excited. When I see the energetic core, I am lost in awe. The energy channels amaze me in their cool way of traversing along, around, and across the body. But the chakras, well, they were just there, swirling, vibrating, humming, but never very captivating to me. What a fool!

I realise now, of course, that this limited connection to the chakra system was because my own chakras were a bit clogged up and out of balance. During my late teens, as I lay in bed, I would sometimes see slight surges through a specific chakra or feel a push from within my chakra system, the same way you may feel a gurgling in your stomach or a twinge in a muscle. But in my ignorance, I was never very interested in the chakras. Well, let me tell you, I have made a 180-degree turnaround on that limited perspective!

I can tell you the day my relationship with chakras changed. I was working with a client who was experiencing some significant limiting patterns in her daily life. She had experienced years of abuse in her childhood home, and although now a woman in her late 30s, she was experiencing unresolved aspects of the trauma of those childhood years that were resurfacing and impacting her relationships. There is a powerful forgiveness prayer from the Hawaiian Huna healing tradition (see the "doing" practice at the end of this chapter), and as we were working, I shared it with her and asked her to begin to say it. At that point, I was simply working with her energy to stabilise the emotions and fears that were running through it, but, by the time she got a few lines into the prayer, I noticed a sudden pushing movement from within her energy system and stepped back.

Her chakra system was moving. At first, her throat chakra restricted to a pinpoint of energy, and then, as if something had leapt in a pool, creating endless ripples of movement, this pinpoint began to ripple and expand, circle after circle, through her throat chakra and the entire area covered by that chakra. These ripples resonated with a vibration filled with sound and colour. As she continued to speak the words of the prayer aloud, even through her tears, the ripples continued constantly and rhythmically releasing, repatterning, and recoding energy patterns throughout. Starting in her throat chakra, they quickly began sending the same patterns through her heart chakra. Once the ripples started there, the whole of her chakra system engaged and started transforming, evolving, releasing, and healing. I have been in love with the chakras since then.

There are seven main chakras within your energy system, and you can think of each one as a hub of energy, each connected

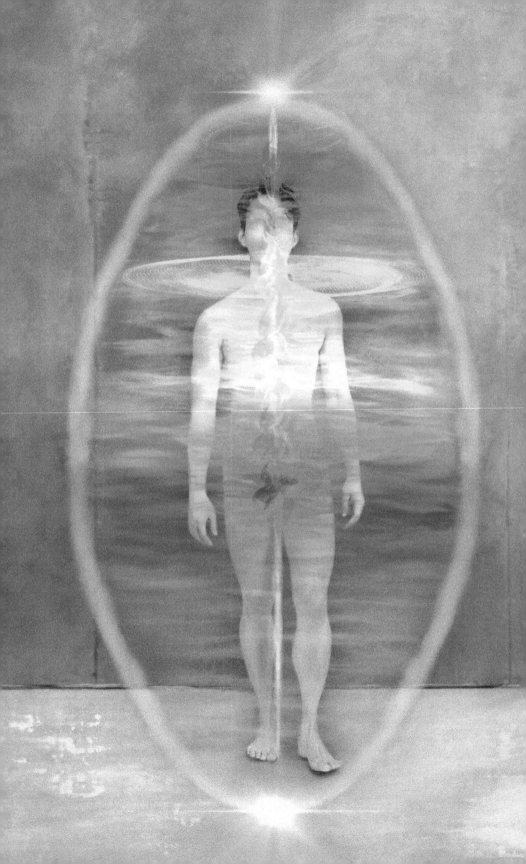

together through a central core. The word *chakra* comes from the Sanskrit word meaning 'disc,' and they are so named because each chakra moves in a horizontal swirling motion like a disc, from the depth of your energetic core to the edge of your auric field.

For a moment, take your mind back to your understanding of your energetic core, the superhighway of energy moving in both directions simultaneously with the *Earth star* beneath your feet and the *Sun star* above your head. Both of these powerful energy centres hold a very different vibration, one of the Earth and one of the Cosmos, and there is a vast vibrational difference between them. Each of your chakras holds the transition from the vibration of matter, physicality, and Earth to the vibration of space, unity, and the Cosmos. Like rungs up and down a ladder, your chakras enable you to activate the potential that is housed in every one of your human cells and manifest it into the world, and therefore into the great web of life.

Let's take a whirlwind visual tour of the chakras. With only one more energy system after this to explore (the heartfield), I want to help you start putting it all together:

1. At your depth is your energetic core, complete with your *Earth star* and *Sun star*, which brings energy in from above and below continuously and simultaneously.

Speaking truth activates your throat chakra and can help bring balance to your entire energy system.

2. Your fabulous point of fusion is where your body system begins to carry your core energy throughout your body, as well as through all other parts of your energy anatomy.

3. At this point of fusion, the chakras begin. A great visual for you to hold in mind is of having seven spinning planets located in your spine, each sitting on top of the next. And not just any planet, but Saturn, with its amazing rings emanating through all of your body (front, back, and sides) and into your aura.

4. Physically, chakras are created by multiple bunches of nerves coming together in seven distinct places in your body. Each of these nerve bunches is called a 'plexus' (you may be familiar with your solar plexus, for example), and each of the seven main ones of your body correlate to a specific chakra. In the chart below, you can read more about each plexus and where it is located in the body.

5. You can think of a plexus as where your physical body meets your energetic core, and that exquisite information and energy begin translating through your whole body system. Each plexus is in a different area of the body, and each informs and is informed by different nerves, organs, muscles, glands, bones, and tissue.

6. Because of where each chakra is housed in your physicality and how it relates to the movement between your *Earth star* and *Sun star*, each chakra has a distinct vibration. This can manifest as a different colour,

moving from the deep, rich red of the root chakra to violet, the highest frequency of light energy our human eyes can see.

7. Each of these parts of your physical anatomy holds cellular, or body memory, and these memories inform the chakras. Likewise, your chakras hold understandings from your amazing core, from your template of health, and from the benefit of being connected to the whole of your body system. You may say that the chakras hold all of your potential for life and are the roadmap for how to help that potential manifest. This energetic information flows into every part of your corresponding physical anatomy, meaning there is a continual flow of information between physical and energetic and energetic and physical.

8. The energy closest to your core holds the deepest information about the way you experience life. This is where ancestral information can inform your body, thoughts, mind, and emotions. The chakra energy farthest away from your core holds information about what has gone on in your day and how it fits into the general theme and understanding of each specific chakra. This information moves from the outer edge of your energy system, in through your lovely lemniscates, to wherever it is most appropriately housed.

Clinically, working with the chakras is an amazing way to affect everything within a body system. Physically, each chakra helps inform, heal, and balance any organ, tissue, or gland

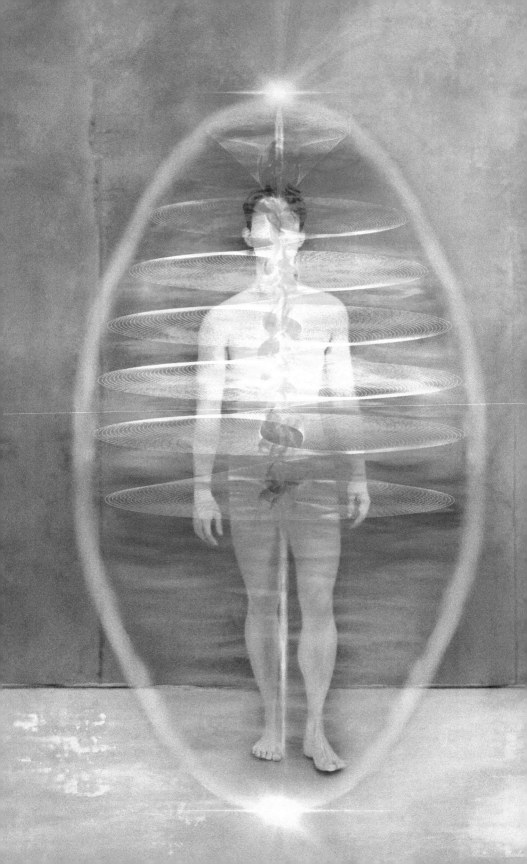

within its area. Energetically, each helps maintain the flow and balance of

- The extraordinary channels that run through that section of your body.

- The organ meridian channels related to that part of your body.

- The electrical circuits of the cells in that area.

- The corresponding area of the aura, either negatively or positively, depending on the health of the chakra.

- Your grounding, stability, resilience, and joy.

- Your life journey of becoming.

Up until this point, I have been talking about the individual chakras, but what is essential to understand about the chakra system is that not only is every individual chakra in its process of inviting balance, but each is communicating with one another to help bring balance to every part of you – physically, emotionally, energetically, and spiritually. Each chakra is responsible for coding, interpreting, and storing information about specific themes, as well as sharing this information with the rest of your energy fields. (This communication is done

Each of your chakras holds the transition from the vibration of matter, physicality, and Earth, to the vibration of space, unity, and the Cosmos.

through those luscious lemniscates I wrote about in a previous chapter.)

Each chakra has an immense responsibility and power, and knowing how to help your chakras balance is a wonderful and powerful way to affect your physical health, your emotional health, and your ability to connect with your fullest life. Below, you'll find a breakdown of each of the seven chakras, including their locations, and areas of governance, and including their related nerve plexi, and also an affirmation to help support that specific chakra. Words have powerful energetic forms, and by consciously working with a life-affirming sentence, you can help unblock your chakras, allowing your energy to again flow freely. I have also put all of the information below in a summary chart at the end of the chapter.

ROOT CHAKRA

- Location: from the top of your thighs to a hand's-width above your pubic bone – front, back, and sides.

- Physical relationship with: the reproductive system, legs, feet, bones, teeth, perineum, pelvis, ovaries, and testes.

- Plexus: sacral-coccygeal.

- Themes: belonging, family, safety, connection.

- Affirmation: *Because I am alive, I belong.*

SACRAL CHAKRA

- Location: one hand's-width below your navel to one hand's-width above your navel – front, back, and sides.

- Physical relationship with: reproductive and genitourinary system (womb, genitals, kidneys, bladder).

- Plexus: sacral.

- Themes: innocence and joy, expression of being, trust, connection.

- Affirmations: *Because I am alive, I have joy* and *I embrace my joy and my curiosity.*

SOLAR PLEXUS CHAKRA

- Location: one hand's-width above your navel to the bottom of your breastbone (sternum) – front, back, and sides.

- Physical relationship with: digestive and metabolic system (stomach, spleen, liver, pancreas, adrenal glands).

- Plexus: solar.

- Themes: identity, individuality, empathy, connection.

- Affirmation: *Because I am alive, I experience.*

HEART CHAKRA

- Location: the bottom of your breastbone to two fingers below your collarbone.

- Physical relationship with: immune system and circulatory system (heart, lungs, pericardium, thymus).

- Plexus: cardiac and pulmonary.

- Themes: passion, compassion, unconditional love, connection.

- Affirmation: *Because I am alive, I love.*

THROAT CHAKRA

- Location: two fingers below your collarbone to the tip of your nose.

- Physical relationship with: respiratory system (throat, neck, arms, thyroid, parathyroid).

- Plexus: pharyngeal.

- Themes: expression, authenticity, truth, connection.

- Affirmation: *Because I am alive, I share my truth.*

BROW CHAKRA

- Location: the tip of your nose to the upper part of your forehead.

- Physical relationship with: endocrine and nervous system (eyes, face, cerebrospinal fluid, pineal, pituitary).

- Plexus: carotid.

- Themes: insight, vision, imagination, connection.

- Affirmation: *Because I am alive, I vision my world into being.*

CROWN CHAKRA

- Location: the upper part of your forehead and the entire top of your head.

- Physical relationship with: central nervous system (brain, spinal cord).

- Plexus: cerebral cortex.

- Themes: spirituality, interbeing, cosmic awareness, peace, connection.

- Affirmation: *Because I am alive, I am an essential part of the great mystery.*

The chakras are unique to your energy system in that they exist at the most superficial levels *and* they travel deep into your energetic core, relaying information through all their concentric layers (remember rings of Saturn!).

One of the primary purposes of your chakra system is to make sense of and interpret your life. It stores the energetic coding of every one of your experiences. Can you imagine that? Your chakra system holds within it *every single* experience you have ever had. Wow! Your energy is amazing!

CHAKRA KEY THEMES

	Location	Physical relationship with	Element	Theme	Affirmation
Root Chakra	From the top of your thighs to a hand's-width above your pubic bone – front, back and sides	Reproductive system. Legs, feet, bones, teeth, perineum, pelvis, ovaries and testes.	Earth and Fire	Belonging, family, safety, connection	Because I am alive, I belong
Sacral Chakra	One hand's-width below your navel to one hand's-width above your navel – front, back and sides	Reproductive and genitourinary system. Womb, genitals, kidneys, bladder	Water	Innocence and joy, Expression of being, Trust, Connection	Because I am alive, I have joy I embrace my joy and my curiosity
Solar Plexus Chakra	One hand's-width above your navel to the bottom of your breast bone (sternum) – front back and sides	Digestive and metabolic system. Stomach, spleen, liver, pancreas, adrenal glands	Fire	Identity, Individuality, Empathy, Connection Affirmation	Because I am alive, I experience
Heart Chakra	The bottom of your breast bone (sternum) to two fingers below your collarbones	Immune system and circulatory system. Heart, lungs, pericardium, thymus	Fire, and the Alchemy of All Elements	Passion, Compassion, Unconditional love, Connection Affirmation	Because I am alive, I love
Throat Chakra	Two fingers below your collarbone to the tip of your nose	Respiratory system. Throat, neck, arms, thyroid, parathyroid	Air	Expression, Authenticity, Truth, Connection Affirmation	Because I am alive, I share my truth
Brow Chakra	The tip of your nose to the upper part of your forehead	Endocrine and nervous system. Eyes, face, cerebral spinal fluid, pineal, pituitary	Air	Insight, Vision, Imagination, Connection	Because I am alive, I vision my world into being
Crown Chakra	The upper part of your forehead and the entire top of your head	Central nervous system. Brain, spinal cord	The Alchemy of all Elements	Spirituality, Interbeing, Cosmic awareness, Peace, Connection Affirmation	Because I am alive, I am an essential part of the great mystery

PRACTICES

 Thinking:
Affirming You, Becoming You

Read the seven affirmations below that correlate with each chakra and really think about what they mean:

1. *Because I am alive, I belong.*

2. *Because I am alive, I have joy.*

3. *Because I am alive, I experience.*

4. *Because I am alive, I love.*

5. *Because I am alive, I share my truth.*

6. *Because I am alive, I vision my world into being.*

7. *Because I am alive, I am an essential part of the great mystery.*

Out of these seven statements, which one most resonates with you? Which one do you least connect to? For example, do you feel that you belong, no matter where you are? Do you feel that you are able to share your truth in any situation?

When you focus your attention on each of these statements, your attention will initiate movement and enquiry within your chakra system. Your cognitive and emotional responses to thinking about these affirmations can guide you towards discovering which chakras hold more and less balance for you.

Once you have identified which chakra you would like to support more, you can bring its affirmation to mind several times a day, which will bring more of that chakra, and your awareness of it, into your daily life. This, in turn, balances the energy in that chakra as well as your chakra system in its entirety.

 Feeling:
Connecting Your Chakras

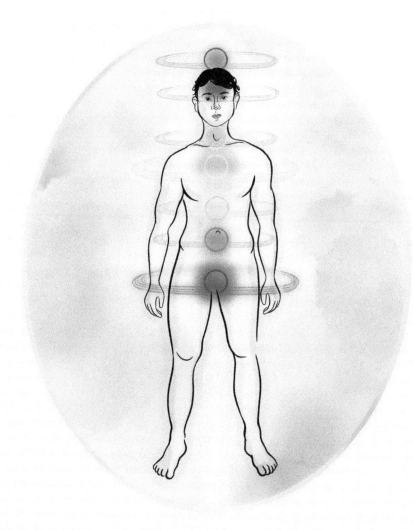

1. Look at the picture of the chakras.

2. Place one hand flat on top of your head and the other flat over your lower abdomen or pubic bone.

3. Take three nourishing breaths.

4. Now, tune into your body and get curious. Keep one hand still on either your crown or your root chakra and move your other hand towards it, one chakra at a time. Which hand are you going to hold still, and which one are you going to move? There is no wrong answer or direction, it simply depends on how your chakra system is at the time and which way is most supporting and balancing for it.

5. Once you get a feeling for whether you are moving up or down your chakra system, keep the one hand supporting either the crown or root chakra while placing your other hand flat on its neighbouring chakra. Take seven relaxing breaths to connect these two chakras before moving onto the next chakra. Continue in this way until both hands are on the same chakra. After your seven breaths with this chakra, give a moment of thanks to your body and life and move on with your day more balanced, grounded, and connected.

Doing:

The Ho'oponopono Prayer

The Ho'oponopono Prayer is based on forgiveness and healing practices of ancient Hawaiians, and this modern form of prayer is an effective and peaceful way to bring significant balance and healing in your energy fields.

The four lines of the prayer can be said in any sequence, but are best said aloud, as energetically, this creates a bridge of consciousness within all aspects of your physical, emotional, and sacred health.

I love you

I am sorry

Please forgive me

Thank you

1. Choose a theme in your life that you wish to evolve towards balance and health. This may be a challenging relationship, a past experience, or even something more internal, such as how you feel about yourself.

2. Begin to say the prayer aloud while focusing your attention on that person or theme you wish to bring healing to.

3. Continue saying the prayer aloud for several minutes.

   Tip: If you are working to bring healing into a specific relationship (whether it is an active and living relationship or a relationship of the past, because that person is either no longer in your life or has died), it is useful to have a photo of that person or something that represents them. This visual prompt can help your energy focus on clearing all limiting patterns of pain and restriction.

Remember, I have created videos of many of the practices in this book, so I can guide you as we do them together. You can find these videos and other supporting material at www.pruneharris.com/radiant-soul.

You who want

knowledge,

seek the Oneness

within. There you

will find

the clear mirror

already waiting.

~Hadewijch II

(1200–1260)

THE HEARTFIELD

Don't let your brain

interfere with your heart.

~Albert Einstein

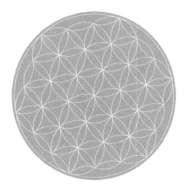

Have you ever been to a play, musical, or concert where there was a live orchestra? I am always amazed to hear the discordant cacophony of noise that occurs as the players and instruments are warming up. Then there is a pause of silence before they begin. All these individuals then put their attention on the waving baton, swinging hands, and moving body of the conductor and follow their will. That conductor's baton is like a magic wand, bringing harmony, organisation, direction, power, and beauty to the vastly different characters of each musician and instrument. Meanwhile, the conductor has all senses tuned to every individual – watching, listening, feeling, noticing everything and responding accordingly, fixing this musician with eye contact, fixing that musician with an extra flamboyant baton movement, and using their whole body to be in a continual exchange of information. And all to create that magnificent piece of music in its fullness of potential.

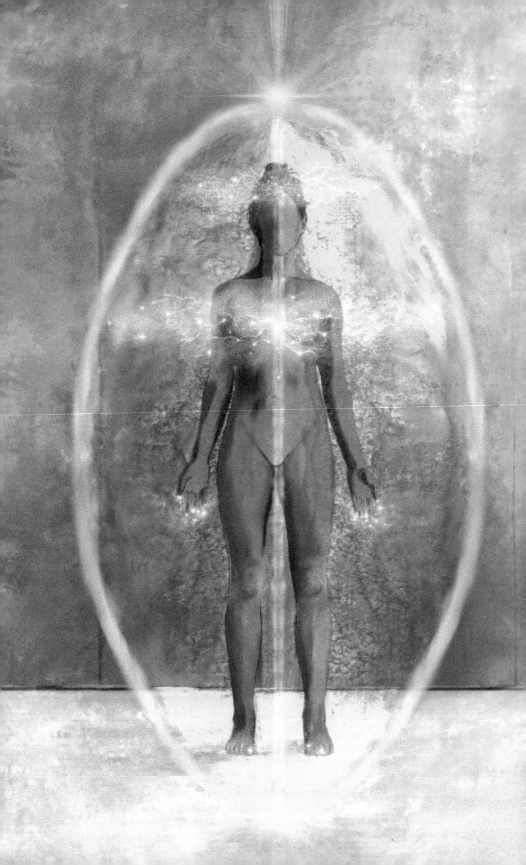

This is exactly what the heart does in your whole body system.

Your heart holds the rhythm, beat, organisation, and direction of your entire energy system. It beats every minute of the day and night. On average, it will beat over 4,000 times in an hour, about 100,000 times a day, and about 365 million times a year. Wow!

THE WISE HEART

We are taught in biology that the heart is a pump. Yes, it pumps blood around our bodies, but it does so much more than that.

Have you ever experienced heartbreak? Pumps don't experience heartbreak; they either work or they don't. Have you ever felt love? Pumps don't experience love; they either work or they don't.

Sometimes I get lost staring at the energy of the valves working in the heart, for they are like tiny, powerful gateways opening and closing. Gateways of information, power, and wisdom; gateways of consciousness and potential; gateways between your physical body and your non-physical body; gateways of everything that you know and everything that you are yet to know. Gateways to more gateways.

←——————————

Your heart empowers your Radiant Soul energy to move through every one of your cells, connecting the head, brain, body and soul continually.

Within your energy fields, your heart is the centre of awareness and consciousness. It is the great receiver, with all other energy systems feeding into it, and it is the great giver, for every other energy system is fed by the energy of the heart.

Energy is full of these sorts of seeming paradoxes, for energy doesn't quite fit into the dualistic concept of life/death, good/bad, giving/receiving. Energy operates beyond dualism because it is always relational. Think of anything to do with energy as being part of a relational exchange. When you understand this, it is perfectly possible for all energy to feed the heart and all energy to flow from the heart to feed every other part of your whole body system. Your heart is in continual communication and information exchange as it monitors, regulates, calms, urges, and acts like the conductor, waving a magic wand so that everything you are can come into being.

One of my favourite quotes about the heart is from 17th century philosopher Blaise Pascal who writes, 'The heart has reason that reason cannot know.'[1] Its energy field carries wisdom, memory, and consciousness.

There are multiple fascinating case studies of when a transplant recipient receives a donor heart and is able to know things about the life of the donor that have never been told to them. In many documented cases, the recipient also

---

[1] Blaise Pascal, *Pensées*, trans. A. J. Krailsheimer (New York: Penguin Classics, 1995).

integrates personality changes that mirror the personality of the donor. This memory transference means that oftentimes the recipients dream in great detail about the donor, enough to know exactly how they died, what they were called, and who they loved.[2] In one of the most high-profile cases, the information shared by an eight-year-old heart recipient provided all the evidence needed to lead to the arrest of the donor's murderer.[3]

Energetically, your heart is the densest organ, and its energy moves in spirals from the top to the bottom and from the bottom to the top. This spiral action enables your heartfield to receive all the energy coming into your energetic core from above your head, and all the energy coming in from below your feet. From that central place, it then holds the rhythm of all your energy systems. But, of course, the heart also has direct physical impact, and none more so than through the blood.

---

[2] Brigitta Bunzel, Brigitte Schmidl-Mohl, Alice Grundböck, and Gregor Wollenek, "Does Changing the Heart Mean Changing Personality? A Retrospective Inquiry on 47 Heart Transplant Patients," *Quality of Life Research* 1, no. 4 (August 1992): 251–256, https://doi.org/10.1007/BF00435634; Paul Pearsall, Gary E. R. Schwartz, and Linda G. S. Russek, "Changes in Heart Transplant Recipients That Parallel the Personalities of Their Donors," *Journal of Near-Death Studies* 20, no. 3 (Spring 2002): 191–206, https://doi.org/10.1023/A:1013009425905.

[3] Sandeep Joshi, "Memory Transference in Organ Transplant Recipients," *Journal of New Approaches to Medicine and Health* 19, no. 1 (April 24, 2011), https://www.namahjournal.com/doc/Actual/Memory-transference-in-organ-transplant-recipients-vol-19-iss-1.html.

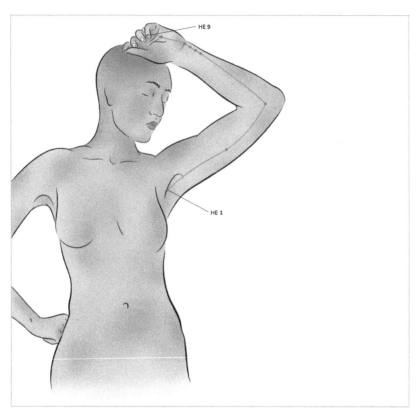

Your heart meridian empowers your loving hugs and healing hands.

YOUR BLOOD VIBRATES WITH LIFE

My dad was a farmer and a butcher; his father and brothers were farmers, butchers, and publicans; and the ancestry through my father's line has been farmers, butchers, and pub owners for many, many generations. (They were also town criers, but that isn't quite so relevant to the story!) I grew up above a town butcher shop, and seeing blood was a very normal experience for me as I walked through the shop or helped serve customers.

I was seven when I went with my mum to feed our cows one day. We were met with one of our cows, Lily, having broken a horn off her head. She was very chilled out and calm about it as she stood there greeting us with her horn hanging, blood all over her face, and a mass of pulp where the horn had joined her head. Mum went to fetch Dad to help remove the horn and dress the wound, so for about an hour, I sat on a wooden bench beside Lily as the blood oozed slowly from her head. Here is what stood out for me:

1. Lily was completely unperturbed by what was going on. She had done something, her horn had broken, that was then, now was now; she was fine.

2. The blood smelt really strong. It vibrated, and it smelt.

3. *It vibrated*? The blood was absolutely packed with energy. In fact, it was packed with *life* energy. Her whole face was buzzing as the blood congealed on her face and head.

As I washed Lily's face, I felt the magnetic energy in her blood. My own hands buzzed with the magnetism of touching it. It was that powerful, that power-packed.

I realised that day just how much life and energy is in blood. Not the dark, dead blood I was used to in the butcher shops, but the vibrant bright-red blood in the living body. Moving through 60,000 miles of veins, arteries, and capillaries, your blood is a river of communication and nourishment. It greets as it goes, giving life force and sustenance as well as cleaning, connecting, and loving every part of your physical body. Yep, loving. Your heart and your blood hold loving consciousness; your heart and blood *are* conscious.

Your body *wants* to be manifest and alive. Your spirit and soul *want* to be manifest and alive. It is no accident that you are alive right now. There are countless stories about the human will to survive despite unbearable odds or in unimaginably difficult situations. The human will to live is a profound and vital thread in the cosmic web of life, and every part of your blood supports your life.

I could write about the wonders of the heart for many, many pages!

Callie came into my clinic gentle, smiling, loving, and so ungrounded that I could see space between the bottom of her energy field and the floor. An artist, she had come because of her pattern of disastrous relationships with men. Time after time, her kindness and generosity were taken advantage of, and she was left broken-hearted and bereft. And yet, she found herself in a similar situation with the next relationship. And the next.

It wasn't only her lack of boundaries or assertiveness that was creating the imbalance, but also a lack of love for herself that showed up in a willingness to accept a relationship without any real or respectful love exchange.

Callie loved the Earth, humanity, animals, people, painting, and cooking. She was deeply loving, but that didn't extend to herself, her body, or her dreams. Being raised to think of others before herself, Callie took that pattern so strongly into her energy fields that she no longer knew how to think of herself, or the reason for doing so. (I wish there were a positive spin on the word 'selfish' in the English language. Being positively selfish is essential. Looking after yourself as well as looking after others means that any relationship can hold mutual respect, compassion, and love, for without being able to respect and love yourself, you simply have no foundational ground for extending those emotions out to other people.)

For the first few sessions, we worked on ways to help her energy field ground itself, for I knew that until that happened, there would be little else that could transform or shift her energy to affect her ability to see, love, and commit to herself. The grounding helped, and after a few sessions, it was holding more. This in itself was affecting Callie's heartfield, as she was now being electromagnetically powered up in a way that had been meagre before.

During our fourth session, I looked to activate her entire heartfield at a different level. There are many ways to do this, but looking at her system I saw it was the organ meridian channels of her heart that looked the most dull and uninspired. There is a powerful plexus at the place where the skull and the spine meet. Sometimes referred to as the 'power point,' or the 'alta major' chakra, it holds a bridging energy between everything physical and energetic above the throat, and everything physical and energetic below the throat. It is deeply electrical and hooked into all parts of the nervous system. I held this point with one hand while connecting into access points of the organ meridian of her heart. It took time: 30 minutes, 40 minutes, 50 minutes . . . but through it all, the meagre energy in the channel was beginning to deepen. Callie slept as I held the point, watching her life force begin to connect once more with her heart organ. At one point, she gave a sudden start and jumped involuntarily, momentarily waking up, only to settle back into sleep again. But that was the jump-start of her electrical system, and it initiated a cascade of light, colour, movement, and connection that poured from her heart into every cell and every energy system, shot into her core, and powered up every part of her being. It was one of the most beautiful energy moments I have ever had the great privilege to witness.

And that was the end of those disastrous relationships. She is now happily married to a wonderful man and, even more importantly, happily in love with herself.

ARE YOU READY TO START PUTTING IT ALL TOGETHER?

I want to give you a visual overview of what the heartfield looks like and how it connects to your other energy systems, for it is complex, intricate, and beautiful.

Everything you are is unique, interconnective and magnificent.

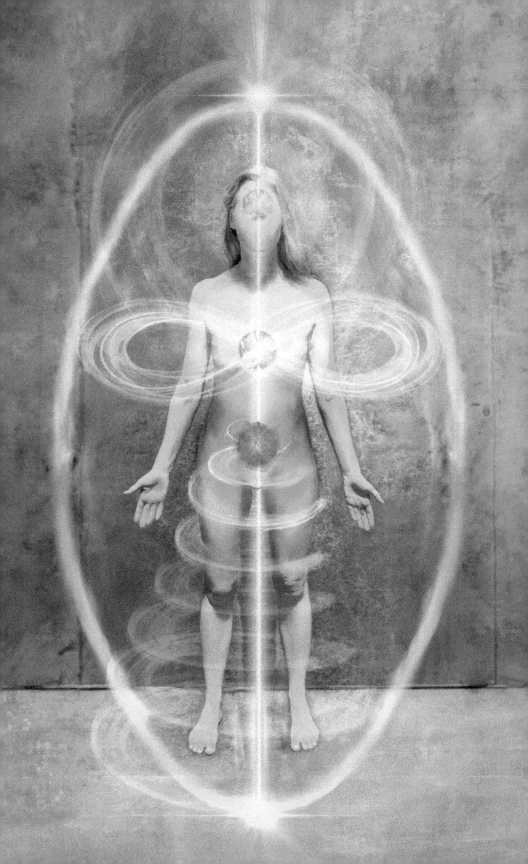

1. Energetic Core Connection

   Energy comes into your energetic core from above your head and below your feet. From this core, there is one key place where your energy gets stored, and that is in an amazing energy centre housed deep in your lower abdomen. The ancient Chinese called this energy centre the lower dantian, and the ancient Celts called it the 'Cauldron of Warming.' You can think of this energy centre as housing all of your physical energy, ready to serve the magnificent potential that is you and your life. This physical and potentially rich energy feeds many of your energy channels and also shoots energy up to your heart area, where it is received by the *middle dantian*, or the 'Cauldron of Calling.' This is the energy that feeds your life path and your soul path and nurtures the longing in your life. Don't think of this longing as something that is unattainable, however. This is the longing that produces your dreams, guides your leaps along your pathway, notices synchronicities, and foments your deep creativity.

2. The Electromagnetic Field of the Heart

   Your heart's electromagnetic field is the connection between the lower and middle dantians that creates either a strong electromagnetic energy field measurable several centimetres off your physical body or a weak electromagnetic field. The more energy moving from your lower dantian to your middle dantian, the more energy feeding through your whole body system, including your magnificent heartfield.

When I teach, I have a habit of going through several microphones a day, as my own heartfield expands to share information with students in the room. This expansion is generally too much for electronic equipment to handle. At the last live class I streamed, I was told by the astounded audio-visual technicians, politely but firmly, that I was not to walk near them at any time after I had crashed their entire streaming system twice simply by getting close to their tables!

3. The Electrics of the Body

   Your heart is the most electrical organ in your body. This has partly to do with the blood, and partly to do with the profound connection between the physical power being released from the lower dantian into each and every one of your cells. You can imagine your cells as being power-packed batteries, each with its own positive and negative charge, all lined up to carry your essential electromagnetic flow through your entire physical and energetic system. Your heart manages this flow.

4. Heart Chakra

   There are a myriad of energy anatomy components to your heartfield aside from the physical organ of the heart, the two dantians, and the electromagnetic field of your heart. You have already read about the heart chakra, and this beautiful energy bathes your entire chest area, informing and being informed by the heart. It is also responsible for helping manage the flow of energy down from your heart into your *Earth star* and up from the heart into your *Sun star*. Your heart is the very centre of your life, your potential, and your becoming.

5. The Deep Heart

    You also have the deep heart, where much of your heart's wounds get tucked away and stored until they can be healed and integrated back into the whole. You might be able to relate to your deep heart through an experience of tension or pain stuck right between your shoulder blades, and no matter what stretches you do, you can't shift it. That is how the deep heart can get you to pay attention to what needs to be healed within the story of your heart.

6. The Assemblage Point

    One of the most exquisite aspects of your heartfield's energy anatomy is the way your heart connects directly into your energetic core, for it is the only part of your distinct energy system that does this. Towards the top of your sternum is a quite amazing energy point, sometimes called the 'high heart' chakra. It is a tiny, dense, whirling storm of energy, and from it emanates long, silver filaments. These filaments come directly from your energetic core and extend out about 30–40 centimetres from your sternum. At the end of these filaments, floating within all the rich, interwoven complexities of your energy fields, is a translucent energy sphere. (Remember the story in Chapter 4, when I described seeing that little boy's soul light shining so brightly? What I was seeing was his assemblage point).

Shamanically, this sphere has long been called 'the assemblage point,' and that is the word I use for it, as it is the point around which your internal and external perceptions assemble.

Your assemblage point is the place where your soul takes in information from your daily life and where your daily life receives information and guidance from your soul. It is the only part of your energy anatomy that has its own protective and communicative energy field separate from the whole. This assemblage point moves around your chest area as you go through your day being aware, being conscious, gathering information, and sharing information. When people talk about following their guiding light, I believe it is this radiant sphere they are referring to, even on a subconscious level.

Wow! There is so much going on in your heartfield, isn't there? Each and every one of these components is beautifully complex and interwoven with the next, and this is just the top-level overview of the heartfield. But at least you get a quick look at just what is going on right now and every second of the day in that space all around your chest. Look down at it right now and be filled with wonder!

PRACTICES

Tracking the Life in Your Veins

Did you know you have 66,000 miles of veins, arteries, and capillaries in your body? Take a few moments today and think about how nourished you are with every beat of your heart. Choose a place to start focusing your thoughts. Maybe it is in your extremities, such as your fingers or your toes, or perhaps it is the very centre, the heart itself. Can you use your thoughts to follow your blood vessels either to or from your heart? Can your thoughts track the way in which every single part of your body is nourished, supported, enquired after, and attended to by your lifeblood?

Feeling:
Expanding the Heart

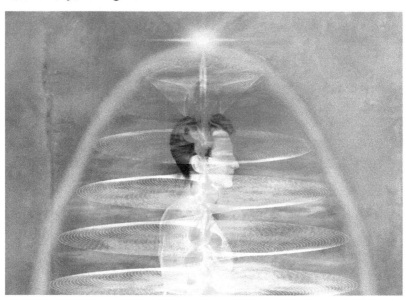

Your heartfield is one of your most immediately responsive energy fields. For a moment, turn your attention to something that makes you sad. Your heartfield has just become a lot smaller around your body. Now think about and feel into something that makes you happy. Your heartfield has just lit up and expanded.

Take three nourishing breaths as you continue to emotionally connect with what makes you happy (maybe *lots* of things/people/places/situations that make you happy). You have just aided your heartfield, your electromagnetic grounding, and therefore everything about your energy systems.

 Doing:
Spiralling the Heart

This is a wonderful practice for clearing electromagnetic and energetic debris from your beautiful heartfield.

1. Place one hand on your chest (it doesn't matter which hand).

2. Begin drawing very small circles with your hand. At first, they can be on your skin and move in whatever direction feels best to you. Whether it feels better to go clockwise or anticlockwise, continue moving your hand in that direction for the entire practice.

3. Increase the size of the circle, and at the same time, begin moving your hand off your body.

4. Continue to circle in the same direction all the way off your body so that your arm is extended out to the edge of your aura.

5. Continue to circle in the same direction all the way back to your body.

6. Repeat as many times as feels good.

Remember, I have created videos of many of the practices in this book, so I can guide you as we do them together. You can find these videos and other supporting material at www.pruneharris.com/radiant-soul.

I have found that the platonic affection in friendships and familial love for children can be relied upon with certainty to lift the bruised soul and repair the wounded spirit.

~Maya Angelou
(1928–2014)

10

YOUR ENERGY,
YOUR POWER

Nothing happens until something moves. When something vibrates, the electrons of the entire universe resonate with it. Everything is connected.

~Albert Einstein

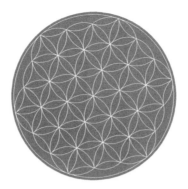

Now that you understand the basics of how your energy systems work, and how to bring in those tiny and profound adjustments to affect the flow and connectivity of these systems, you have far more access to the fullness of yourself. Nowhere in your world do you have to be a victim. Nowhere do you have to settle for anything that isn't part of your unique life path. You have a choice in all situations, but to engage in this choice, you need to have energy and feel empowered.

Can you think of anything that has happened in the last few days that you felt a dip of energy around? Something that knocked you off balance a bit or made you feel upset or wobbly?

It may have been an interaction with someone close to you, such as a spouse, parent, or sibling, or something that happened at work. When you think about it now, does it still affect you, or do you feel absolutely no charge as you reflect on it? If you still experience some emotion around it, then that emotion indicates there is still an imbalance in your energy field about it; on some level, this experience has created power loss or fed into a previous energetic software glitch in your system around this issue.

Many years ago, I realised that in every sentence where the word 'energy' is used, it could be interchanged with the word 'power.' At the time, this was a pretty profound realisation for me, as it produced a subtle but important shift in my understanding of energy. It is important to note that the use of the word 'power' here refers to balanced power, not imbalanced power or power *over* someone or something else.

Let's play with that for a while:

- I just don't have any energy today.
  I just don't have any power today.

- Each time we meet, I feel like he sucks my energy away.
  Each time we meet, I feel like he sucks my power away.

- I feel full of energy this morning.
  I feel full of power this morning.

- My energy totally slumped when I watched the news last night.
  My power totally slumped when I watched the news last night.

- After my walk on the beach today, I felt so energised.
  After my walk on the beach today, I felt so powerful.

- The national grid supplies energy to 60 million people.
  The national grid supplies power to 60 million people.

WHEN YOU LOSE YOUR ENERGY, YOU LOSE YOUR POWER

In my clinic, the single constant that was present for every client was power loss. (Remember that 'energy' and 'power' are interchangeable, so you could read this as, 'the single constant that was present for every client was energy loss.') Perhaps this power loss was due to childhood experiences, a recent accident, or a challenging personal or professional relationship, but *any* experience that in some way created disturbances in their energetic patterns resulted in them being able to access less than their natural, true, and full energy.

Why? Remember, your energy systems are designed to be coherent and cohesive, continually sharing and responding to your template of health. When you experience something you don't have resilience around, parts of your energy system will take the hit and can send waves of disorganisation and dissonance throughout your entire energy field. This is energy (or power) loss, for at this point, you no longer have access to your full health, vitality, and consciousness.

Furthermore, this disorganisation and dissonance will create some areas of weakness and depletion in your energy fields. Over two thousand years ago, Greek philosopher Aristotle helped us understand that nature abhors a vacuum, and it is the same with your energy fields. This means that when something happens in your daily life that knocks your energy off balance, there has to be an immediate response within your energy systems. This response is wise and perfect. It keeps you going, it keeps you safe, it keeps you alive. BUT! It doesn't necessarily mean you are able to thrive in your full vitality and consciousness. So, little by little, the knocks of life add up until you are living a much, much smaller version of yourself than is your natural birthright. The saddest factor in all this, though, is that often, you may not even notice.

Power loss can be dramatic and traumatic. Situations such as sudden violence, the unexpected death of a loved one, an accident that affects your physicality, abuse, witnessing or being involved in a natural disaster or an unnatural one, such as an act of terrorism . . . there are so many ways you could experience a trauma that I am not going to list them all here. I truly hope you have no personal experience of trauma, but it is highly likely that if you are at the age to be reading this book, then you have experienced trauma on some level.

But power loss doesn't have to occur as a result of a dramatic and traumatic event. Most power loss is insidious and, as I mentioned earlier, oftentimes goes undetected. Little by little, the flow of your energy/power gets disrupted, and your immense, vibrant, radiant core gets a little more suppressed inside your deep systems, no longer emanating out into your every cell, every day. There are a myriad of everyday situations that lead to continual small amounts of energy/power being lost, and this accumulation of energetic disruption can create a lasting effect on your ability to access the fullness of your life.

Perhaps a lot of your power loss has nothing to do with anyone else. It may have been when you looked in the mirror or played out a pattern or phrase in your mind, telling yourself something judgemental or unkind. When you hear that voice in your head, playing out a programme that you gathered in your growing years – perhaps one that says that you aren't quite good enough – it is because energetically, this information is programmed into your energy fields. It isn't a truth, but as you grew, you began to take this in as an accepted way of thinking about yourself. This, in turn, can solidify in your energy system, becoming like a programme glitch that keeps repeating something negative and disempowering and leading to a disconnect with the true energy, power, and beauty of your life. It is at times like this that words like 'life purpose' or 'soul path' can have little meaning, for you feel like you are living an automated life, running through the same daily experiences again and again as if your life is simply on repeat.

A vital consideration when thinking of energy/power loss is that everything that happens in your energy fields affects your physicality. It may take a while, but any energy pattern of imbalance, when experienced for long enough, will manifest in the densest of your energy fields: your body. Therefore, power loss can express itself as chronic illness, anxiety, depression, simmering resentment, anger, or a variety of other symptoms.

Let's take, for example, the current global situation. How empowered do you feel regarding the environmental, social, and political situation that surrounds you? When you perceive aspects of the dysfunctional chaos that is ever-present in our world, do you feel like you are an active part of the creative solutions that will change the world for you, your loved ones, and your descendants? Or do you feel disempowered, helpless, and, on the darkest days, hopeless?

When you have access to your energy, whether you are living your big life or your small life, each step you take is on your evolving life path, created in that place of exquisite connection between your consciousness, your soul, and the great web of life you live within. Another way of saying this would be the evolving pathway that is created between your soul and the soul of the world. So for you to be living your magnificence, you have to have energy; you have to have power.

For you to be living your magnificence, you have to have energy, you have to have power.

The great news is that your whole body system is designed to be continually powered up with every breath and with every step – literally. This big, beautiful planet that we are such an integral part of has a very specific electrical and magnetic energy system created both from deep within its core and from far into space with the energy of the Sun. It is this dynamic energy system of the Earth that is designed to continually recharge you as part of life on the planet, every second of the day. Your own energy fields are deeply dependent and respondent to the Earth's energy.

As we navigate our way through a brief exploration of how the magnetic/electrical energies of Earth and space influence you, I want you to keep in mind a simple image of a series of four different-sized batteries:

1. At the smallest level, each of your cells is a *tiny*, power-packed battery.

2. Your human body is a *mid-sized*, power-packed battery.

3. The Earth is a *big*, power-packed battery.

4. The universe is *a gigantic*, power-packed battery.

THE POWERFUL UNIVERSE

You are solar powered. The Sun continually emits massive magnetic charges in the form of electrified gas that blasts towards Earth at a rate of two million miles an hour. These solar winds are a continuous flow of plasma, are composed mostly of electrons and protons, and contain the energy of 40 billion atomic bombs. All this energy/power careens towards Earth with highly specific effects on the planet and all its living organisms, including you.

Because of the vastness of this solar energy, the Earth protects itself (and you) by having its own magnetic field, known as the 'magnetosphere.' This magnetosphere is formed by the interaction of solar wind with Earth's magnetic fields. It is an exquisite meeting point and interface of different energy, just as when you meet up with a friend and your two energy fields interact to create a unique meeting point you get with only that specific friend. If there were no magnetosphere, the energy of the Sun would instantaneously blow up Earth, so we can think of it very much like the protective aura of the Earth. And just like the human aura, the Earth's aura is responsible for connection and communication, allowing energy, mass, and momentum to be transferred from the solar winds to regions inside the planet's magnetosphere.

So, we have this amazing solar energy blasting towards us, along with the continual buffer of the magnetosphere. But just as you can have sparky relationships and discussions with friends where creativity abounds, the meeting point of space and Earth systems creates huge amounts of energy, especially when the Sun is being particularly active and sending out massive solar flares. This meeting point is called the 'ionosphere.' The universe, and energy in general, continually seeks balance, so the ionosphere channels all this extra energy into clouds. And then what happens? Lightning! This energy moves from cloud electricity straight into Earth in the form of five thousand lightning strikes that hit every minute (five thousand a minute, every minute, every day, every night!). That still just blows my mind. Lightning creates a massive electrical current that lasts just a fraction of a second, producing a strong magnetic field that creates and releases free electrons. These free electrons bob around over the entirety of Earth's crust and, when your energy is in a place to receive this natural and powerful energy, straight into you to empower your every breath, thought, emotion, and physicality.

When I think about the human electrical system, I get very excited. It is a marvel; it is total; it is impossible to separate from other energetic systems, yet it feels and looks so very different. This is mainly because of its dense vibration. Electrical and electromagnetic energies are different from subtle energy in that they can be measured. And human beings are dense.

We are physical, we can touch and be touched, and all of this is because of our electromagnetic energy.

POWERFUL YOU

Within your body are multiple different electrical systems. There are over 30 trillion living cells in your body, and every one of them operates as a miniature battery, constantly transmitting and receiving energy. Each type of cell has a different internal frequency range in which it operates. Every thought, action, and behaviour is electrical. And all these electrical fields are working simultaneously, from the tiny cell-to-cell connection to the great organising energy field that acts as the master energy field for the whole body system. This organising field, held deep within your energetic core, manifests as the heartfield reaching out from your core, through your entire body, out into your aura, and even past your aura to connect with other living beings. This is a field of resonance and coherence. Wow!

You are an amazing interconnective electrical energy field vibrating with empowered consciousness and wisdom.

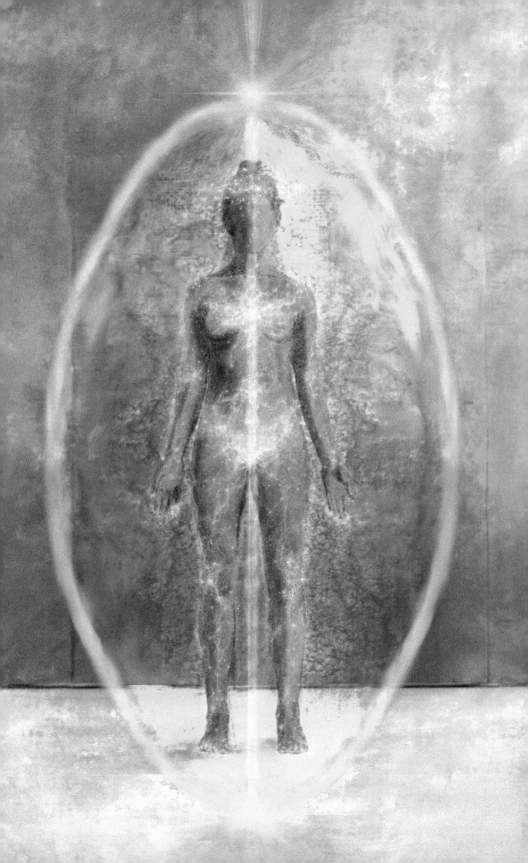

Working with the human electrical system directly affects your

- Heart (and thus everything physical, emotional, and spiritual).

- Brain.

- Bones.

- Fascia.

- Immune system.

- Digestive system.

- Respiratory system.

- Endocrine system.

- *Every* system!

Think of a series of Russian nesting dolls. At the outer layer you have your aura, then your physical body held by your heartfield that extends into your aura, then your nervous system for communication and connection. You have a thin layer of connective tissue, called the *fascia*, that surrounds every individual part of your physical anatomy. So, for example, each of your muscles, organs, bones, nerve fibres, and blood vessels are wrapped in the fascia, and through that thin layer, electrical impulses are continually being created. These piezoelectrical impulses are an amazing component of your electrical system that convey information and energy through your entire body, right down to the tiniest 'Russian doll' of the electricity of a single cell. (And just to blow your mind even further, inside that single cell are electrical and magnetic fields on subatomic particles.)

Your entire electrical energy system is dependent on renewal via the electrics of the Earth and the heavens. Being connected to the energy of the Earth is your way of recharging, of plugging in, in exactly the same way you would plug in your phone to recharge its battery. And you are hardwired to plug in! Everything about your electrical energy system invites this connection and revitalisation. Every single energy system we explored in the previous chapters plays a vital role in holding you strong, stable, and connected into the Earth's energy.

Your energy channels bring electrons into your feet, your aura sucks them into your biofield to be absorbed by your body, your human electrical system carries them through every cell, and your lower dantian takes its power from the amount of Earth energy in your body. All together, your electrical system empowers every function of your body and enables your heartfield to do its job of being that amazing conductor of your entire physical and energetic orchestra.

It is so easy for you to recharge your own electrics and recharge your own battery. You simply need to be grounded electromagnetically and able to receive the abundant electrons that blanket the Earth. Remember how I said that in my clinical practice it was usually only a small shift in a client's energy system that needed to slide into place to create a profound difference? Being grounded electromagnetically was usually the single most important energetic change that empowered that shift.

35-year-old Claire looked rather sheepish as she sat in my clinic for the first time. We had been talking about what she wanted from the sessions and our work together. She had listed some areas of pain in her body, such as acne and recurrent urinary tract infections, but it was apparent in the way her energy fields were moving that there was something more. I waited.

'Actually,' she said, 'I can't really tell you why I'm here. I just know there is something more. Something that I'm missing in my life, and I think you can help.'

As she spoke, her energy fields leapt, cascading into an explosion of colours and radiance. Wow. The beauty and power of her soul shouted its desire to be lived, daily and wonderfully.

Claire was a successful businesswoman with her own business, lived in a nice apartment, and had some great friends, yet she described her life as if she hadn't taken a big breath in years.

'I just know there is more.' Yes, there was. On every level. As I sat looking at her for a long time, I noticed her energy fields were primed for her to live her rich, immense, messy, complicated, full life. When I am deeply tracking energy, I am scanning using two questions: what are the strengths in this person's energy fields, and where are the challenges in this person's energy fields?

The strengths in Claire's system were huge. It was apparent she had done a lot of self-work with regular meditation, consciousness, and connectedness work. Shadows of old patterns of dysfunction had been resolved into balance. Her core energy was magnificent, her energy channels moved well, for the most part, her aura was good, and she was grounded. There was a slight pain and pattern through her heart, as if she needed to heal the final places of a broken love. It was clear there was too much sugar in her system for it to regulate as it was looking to do, hence the infections and acne, but that would be easily balanced. Apart from that, there wasn't much out of balance. I looked closer, scanned deeper, and noticed something almost imperceptible: her energy patterns were moving up more than they were moving down. Despite looking grounded, some kind of imbalance was there.

Simply taking my consciousness to Claire's grounding system helped it present in a different way. I saw the slight energetic imbalance in her heart system flare up, showing itself to be deeper than it originally looked, like a scar that had been opened a few times. The flare of energy initiated a retreat of her grounding system and had a destabilising effect throughout her whole body system. It was subtle but distinct. I had a meaningful starting point.

When I asked Claire if she was in a relationship, she answered, 'No.' She had been in and out of one with a colleague, and although he was great fun and she enjoyed being with him, he was untrustworthy and had cheated on her a few times. She still had feelings for him but was not prepared to settle for a relationship in which there was no trust or deep respect, so she had ended it. As she spoke, the colours of her soul again flared through her energy system, showing that this was a woman who valued herself and knew herself to be worthy, simply because she existed. And yet there was power loss around the pain of being cheated on. It prevented this deep knowledge of her own self-worth from accessing all parts of her energy system and being fully present in her life. She went on to say that it had really knocked down her confidence about being in another relationship.

The only work we did was to increase her groundedness. I knew that if she could connect deeper into the amazing, rejuvenating, and restorative energy of the Earth, her energy system would do the rest, clearing the still-present pain of being betrayed. And with that pain healed, she could bring in deep nourishment so that sugar was no longer an attractive quick fix.

When Claire came to see me a month later, she was radiant – absolutely power-packed. She radiated the kind of joyful and compassionate power that reaches across rooms and lights everyone up. Her skin was clearer, she was free of pain and sugar, and she hadn't had a bladder infection all month. But there was more; I could see it written all over the energy of her heart.

After our session, Claire had taken a week off and spent much of it walking and sitting in nature. During this time, she had a long talk with her heart, and the understandings that had come forward had resulted in her and her long-time best friend taking their relationship to the level of life partner.

'I don't know why I couldn't see it before,' she said. 'I feel like it was always meant to be, but maybe it just came down to the right timing for both of us.'

Needless to say, she didn't need to come back and see me again! Her deeper groundedness had empowered her to not only find her full health, but follow the wisdom of her heart so that she could fully live the life she was here to live.

Research has shown that when you are grounded electromagnetically, the electrons that enter your body do amazing things:

- Increase vitality.

- Reduce stress.

- Balance the nervous system.

- Improve sleep quality.

- Reduce inflammation in the body.

- Reduce or eliminate chronic pain.

- Improve blood pressure and flow.

- Aid cardiovascular health.

- Relieve muscle tension and headache.

- Accelerate healing time.

- Protect the body against e-smog and potentially harmful electromagnetic fields.

In short, being electromagnetically grounded enables your energy system to do its job of keeping you healthy, empowering you to live the life you are here to live.

Your ability to live your fullest life depends on the electromagnetic grounding of your entire energy system.

LET'S GET YOU GROUNDED!

In essence, all you have to do to get grounded is get outside and allow your energy system and the energy system of the Earth to do what they are designed to do. There are, however, many things you can do to increase just how much your energy system can plug in and recharge in the time you have to do so:

1. Be as close to the Earth as you can. Electrons leap through your skin, so physically touching the natural world fast-tracks your recharge. This may be walking barefoot on the ground, lying with your bare arms on the grass, planting trees, smelling flowers up close and personal, giving a tree a long loving hug, or swimming in the ocean.

2. Be conscious of what is occurring. Even if you are walking through a busy city street, you are still in nature. You are breathing air that is rich with energy and walking on paving stones that are abundant with electrons looking to connect with you. Think about what is happening as you are walking through the street or sitting on a park bench. Your consciousness will increase your connectivity and aid the process. If you are stressed and non-conscious as you walk through those streets, you will still take in electrons, but you will be using up their energy as quickly as you are receiving it.

3. Be in gratitude for the process. Nothing aids the balance and health of your entire energy system, including being electromagnetically grounded, more than the energy of gratitude. Gratitude expands your energy fields and helps them reconnect, heal, and grow in their balance and power. As the poet and mystic Rumi wrote so many centuries ago, 'Wear gratitude like a cloak and let it feed every corner of your life.'[1]

By the way, in the time it took you to read this chapter, there have been about 100,000 lightning strikes to provide your body with a continuous power source. You live in an immensely friendly and beneficent universe that empowers you every second of the day.

---

[1] Original source unknown; found at Leah Hall, "58 Short Gratitude Quotes to Bring Meaning to Every Day," CountryLiving, last modified October 27, 2022, https://www.countryliving.com/life/g28564406/gratitude-quotes/.

PRACTICES

 Thinking:
Your Scale of Power

1. Think about a time when you felt most empowered and energised. It may be recently, or perhaps it has been a while since you felt like that. Scan through your life to find when it was that you felt most energised and empowered. Rate that amount of empowered energy as your '100 percent.'

2. Now, scan through your life and think about when you have felt least empowered and energised. Rate that amount of energy as your 'one percent'.

3. Assess your energy and power where you are right now at this exact time in your day. Are you up close to your 100 percent or down closer to your one percent? If you are at anything less than 80 percent, get curious about what you can do, right now, to nourish your own energy. Do you need to take a short walk or sit down on the ground? Do you need to eat some empowering food or pick up the phone for a laugh with a friend? Do you need to do an energy practice from one of the previous chapters? What will empower and energise you right now?

It is my greatest wish for you to never, ever settle for feeling less energised and less empowered than you are able to in any given moment. You are magnificent. You are essential. Be you.

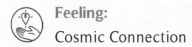 **Feeling:**
Cosmic Connection

When you are feeling low in energy or power, remember that your energetic core is always stable, strong, and immense in its energy. The superficial can be much more variable depending on what the day and your thoughts bring, so use this practice to connect to your core and tap into much more of your true strength and power.

1. Stand up and bring both hands to your chest centre. Take three nourishing breaths and tune into how you feel.

2. Stretch your arms above your head, holding them open to receive the solar power of the Sun.

3. Consciously and actively receive the universal energy from above as it pours into your whole body system.

4. Still standing, lower your arms until your hands are about 50 centimetres away from your thighs; stretch your palms towards the Earth.

5. Consciously and actively receive the Earth energy from below as it pours into your whole body system.

6. You can further increase your energetic connectiveness by stretching one hand up and one hand down, alternating sides to bring in an activating stretch and to create more space in your whole body system.

7. Relax and repeat this sequence until you feel more energised and empowered.

 Doing:
The Gift of Earth Energy

Put this book down and go outside. Sit or lie with as much of your body touching the natural world as you can. Invite yourself to stay where you are for at least 10 minutes. With each inhalation, consciously breathe in the magnificent bounty of Earth energy, and with each exhalation, breathe out gratitude for the Earth. Simple, energising, and powerful.

Regardless of

what barriers confront you,

it is in your power to

free yourselves;

you have only to want to.

~Olympe de Gouges

(1748–1793)

11

LIVING YOUR
BIG LIFE

Live life to the fullest. You have to colour outside the lines once in a while if you want to make your life a masterpiece. Laugh some every day. Keep growing, keep dreaming, keep following your heart. The important thing is not to stop questioning.

~Albert Einstein

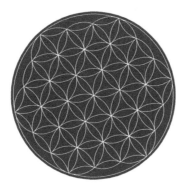

In previous chapters, we explored the six distinct systems of your amazing energy anatomy, as well as how understanding your energy enables you to shatter the illusion of limitation. Everything about your energy fields serves you in your journey of becoming; they are your fields of consciousness and carry connectiveness at every level. Your energy fields enable you to live every step of your life. When you understand how to support them to evolve in balance, you get to choose whether you live your big life or your small life and truly choose to release your fullness, rather than continually hit obstacles or roadblocks on your path of becoming you.

You have a birthright to feel like you are living the life you came here to live. Your birth was not an accident or a cosmic hiccup. It isn't the case that you simply plopped out onto the Earth, and one day you'll die with no effect on the universe. You are an essential part of all of creation. You make up part of this vital, creative, and empowered web of life, and not just any old part that can be replaced or improved upon. No one but you has quite the same vibration, the same essence, the same dreams, the same body or soul. Your thread in this web of life is exquisitely, uniquely, and essentially yours.

I will say it again: You are essential, exactly as you are, with all of your fears and pains and with all of your gifts and beauty. You are part of what makes up this beautiful world, and in every second of every day and every night, you belong. I can't even write that you have a 'right' to belong, because it is beyond rights; it is cosmic law. You are part of the universe; therefore, you belong. Simple. Easy. True.

Can you identify your own magnificence? Can you shine it out into the world? Understanding your energy empowers you to have real choice about who you choose to be. In other words, right now, are you living your small life or your big life?

←————————

You are essential, exactly as you are. Can you identify your own magnificence and shine it out into the world?

WHAT DOES YOUR BIG LIFE LOOK LIKE?

Have you been curious about what it is that you are here to do with your life? Have you asked the question that activist and educator Gigi Coyle invites you to ask: 'What is mine to do?'[1]

Perhaps you are here to hold the light of kindness for others to be inspired by. Perhaps you are here to be a loving parent and nurture the human race in so being. Maybe you are here to promote radical thought. Maybe you are here to inspire the warrior spirit in others, nourish the animal world, talk to the land, or live your big and magnificent quiet life or your big and magnificent shouty-loud life.

What does your big life look like? What changes would occur in your daily life if you were to be living in your fullness, every day, with no patterns of limitation holding you back, no old stories whispering into your heart and mind, no restrictions on how to fully express yourself?

That is my definition of your big life: that you can fully express yourself in all of your magnificence as you walk through your world, every day of your life. Only *you* are discovering what it is you are here to do and here to be.

---

[1] Charles Eisenstein, "Gigi Coyle: What is Mine to Do? (Episode 42)" November 5, 2019, in *A New and Ancient Story*, produced by Charles Eisenstein, podcast, MP3 audio, 1:21:07, https://charleseisenstein.org/podcasts/new-ancient-story-podcast/gigi-coyle-what-is-mine-to-do-e42/.

YOUR TEMPLATE OF HEALTH

Each of your six energy systems is held together in coherence. So, for example, one chakra couldn't simply drop out of place and end up somewhere else in your body system. Nor could a meridian cease to exist. They are cohesive and coherent. There is an organising principle at play in your whole energy fields, and this is what I call your 'template of health.'

I remember the first time I taught about the template of health. I was in a room full of students and practitioners, teaching about specific acupoints in the body that help release more of your deep, essential energy – your soul energy – through your physical body. These points are excellent for when someone has been chronically ill or is beginning to despair over never feeling a connection with their soul path. After talking about how these points are powerful activators of the template of health, I went to move on to my next point, when a man in his 60s, a long-term student of mine who is an excellent practitioner, raised his hand.

'What is the template of health?' he asked.

I was stopped in my tracks. What? I began casually explaining what it was, thinking everyone in the room fully understood what I meant. The participants were furiously scribbling down what I wrote. 'You do all know what I'm talking about?' I asked.

'No,' was the answer across the room. No one had an understanding of the template of health.

'What are you working to activate when you work with your clients?' I asked.

They replied, 'Healing. Balance. Reprogramming energy. Repatterning back to health. Vitality. Energy flow . . . '

'No, those are the *results* of what you are working with,' I said. 'What are you working to *activate* when you work with your clients?'

They understood my question and realised they were working to activate their client's templates of health; they just didn't have the language or understanding to word it in that way.

Running through every part of your energy fields is coding that helps you fully express all of your potential and all of your essence. And this is the profound power in being able to understand your energy. *Anything* and *everything* has the potential to activate your template of health so that it floods your body to clear an imbalance held in your chakras here, to connect a depleted part of your aura there, to move away from stress response . . . to enable you to live your fullest life.

When you are stressed, realise it, and stop to take a deep breath, you are activating your template of health. When you walk through nature and begin to feel more connected, relaxed, and joyful, this is because your template of health has activated more strongly and your body is vibrating differently because of it. When you are with your beloveds who always see your beauty, their witnessing of your essence invites your own template of health to shine more brightly through your whole body system.

When you feel proud of yourself for something, show yourself kindness, laugh with joy, feel love, feel beloved (the list can go on and on), your template of health gets activated just a little bit stronger and vibrates through your whole body system, inspiring your physical health, your emotional health, and your sacred connectedness.

Every living being has this template of health, and although yours is unique to you, it is also part of the morphogenic field that you share with the entire human race. This field is what taps into and creates a collective consciousness, as well as what keeps you operating physically, emotionally, and cognitively. At one exquisite point in time, your conception happened. No matter what the physical experience of that conception was, on the sacred level, it was a moment when your light came into being and the egg and sperm came together to create and activate a new life: you. At this point, you were made of just one cell. Now, you are made of more than 30 trillion. But at that point of conception, and for about 30 hours afterwards, you are just one cell packed with brilliant potential and coding for exactly how to develop in the most perfect way for your soul needs. After 30 hours, that cell divides into two, creating the channel of your energetic core and bringing the expression of your template of health into every place of division. This is the first division of yin *and* yang in your body. Your cells continue to divide from two to four, from four to eight, and so on, until you are 30 trillion cells, all created in a determined and beautiful package coming down the birth canal and into the world. And in every place of division, your template of health gives your energetic fields organisation, cohesion, and coherence.

This, in turn, gives your physical body organisation, cohesion, and coherence.

How do I know? Because I track energy. And when I track energy, this is what I see.

Your template of health is in every meeting point in your body – where a cell meets a cell, where a bone meets a muscle, where an organ meets its surrounding tissue.

There are three distinct places in your body where I see the densest concentration of your template of health: the interface where your energetic core meets your physical body, the interface where your skin and aura meet, and the interface where your aura ends and the outside world begins.

At every interface, your template of health sings with possibility and potential, and so does everybody else's. It is the consciousness of potential that exists in every moment of your life.

THE MAGIC MEETING POINT

How do you meet and engage in the potential of your template of health? Through understanding your energy, for your energy fields are fields of consciousness. 'Consciousness' can be defined as your awareness of your own internal states as well as the events going on around you. Energetically, consciousness means active engagement with the relational aspect of every part of your life. It means you don't just automatically react with a specific habitual action, thought, or emotion; you choose how to *respond*, rather than *react* out of habit. This is the difference between engaging in the conscious parts of your mind, your energy, and your life, and simply allowing your programmed habits to walk through your life for you as if you are walking in your sleep or in a trance.

Another way to describe consciousness is being aware of the space within all meeting points and engaging in the creative potential inherent in that space. This is the point of connectivity that your energy fields move towards in every interaction or energy exchange that you experience. We could call this the cosmic template of health, and it is active at every interface point.

As fields of consciousness, your energy systems engage with and are informed by both your conscious thoughts and your subconscious thoughts. Your subconscious thoughts are the operating programmes that are at play to keep you functioning. They are the habits you form from processing life and how to operate within the confines of your unexplored assumptions.

WHEN BELIEFS TURN INTO HABITS

Why is all of this so important to explore in a chapter called 'Living Your Big Life'? Because your beliefs and unexplored assumptions affect everything about your energy, which means everything about your life, for just as your thoughts follow your energy, your energy follows your thoughts.

This is always one of the most difficult understandings to wrap your head around, and it can be very confusing if you approach life from a dualistic 'this or that'/'one thing or another' perspective. Although, I think by now, you are already well-versed in understanding that nothing is quite so simple or dualistic when it comes to your energy and the way it both continually interacts with, affects, and creates your experiences *and* is affected and created by your experiences.

Understanding your energy and how to help balance it means you can continually support the bridge between your subconscious thoughts and your conscious thoughts, and this empowers you with choice in every situation.

Your subconscious holds all of your unexplored assumptions as well as all of your habitual ways of thinking, being, and doing that you have never questioned, never explored, and possibly never even been curious about. For example, it may be an unconscious assumption that to earn money, you have to work hard and push yourself, continually informing your work ethic and what you are prepared to endure to create your definition of 'success' in your work life. Or it may be an assumption that being a size eight means people will treat you differently and life will be more beloved, easier, and more satisfying than being a size 18. Or perhaps you think you have to be good to be deserving or that you need to have a partner in order to feel fully complete in your life. Maybe you believe you aren't good enough, smart enough, good-looking enough, or brave enough, and that you don't quite belong.

Joshi sat in my clinic with his immense energy field rolling in waves of deeply rich purple. He worked in the corporate world as a facilitator of transformation and leadership and explained that he had recently been promoted into a higher executive team that was challenging him on every level. He said he felt like an imposter and that all the others on the team were much more suited to the role than he was. Joshi held his heart close as he said he felt like he was pretending he had a right to be there and was fearful he would be found out and exposed for who he really was.

It was clear to me who he really was. His energy fields buzzed with health, vitality, wisdom, and gentleness. They were touched at every level by his conscious interaction with his deep dreams and awareness; in other words, this was a person who flowed between their soul and their daily life. I could see that he had worked closely with himself over the years to get to a deep place of balance and that he lived his soul purpose forward with every step. He was inspirational and courageous, and it was this willingness to explore the places where his system moved out of balance that brought him to work with me.

As Joshi talked about feeling like an imposter, I watched the waves of health and vitality moving in his creative field ground to a halt and the habitual field move in, closing down the generous movement and immense connectivity that was so natural to his overall way of being. Everything about his system contracted into fear and loneliness, and separation occurred where just moments before there was cohesion and connection.

There is a fascinating paradox when working with a system that knows itself as well as Joshi's did, for it is always so immensely willing to balance and be whole. And yet, when my clients have done a lot of self-work, the places they tend to show up with are the deep sticking places they have been bumping up against for a long time, usually since childhood or even earlier.

I knew the way to really invite change in Joshi's system and initiate deep healing in his sense of belonging was through inviting a deeper connection with the web of life. Everyone is continually in exchange with energy (and therefore information) in the web of life, and Joshi's energy was used to being in this level of conscious connection.

We planned to work for a day, visiting sacred sites to align his energy to the deeper pulsing of *Earth energy*.

It felt to me that, at a deep place of wounding, he needed to remember that as a human being, he belonged, no matter where he was, who he was with, or what role he was being called to stand within.

We spent a powerful day being with sacred sites close to my home in Cornwall. After aligning more deeply with the beauty and power of nature, we worked in my outdoor clinic beside a stream and under an ancient beech tree. I began to work with the energy of his energetic core. As I held the points on his body that activated deep alignment within his core, I saw the stories of his childhood as they flashed through my awareness: his abandonment as a small boy, his exile from his birth country to the UK and distant family, his experiences of racism and bullying. Turmoil, strife, and uncertainty ran through his childhood and adolescence. The image of a lost child always having to look over his shoulder, and the huge burden of those experiences, still presented deep in his heart despite his inner work and desire to heal.

And through it all, Joshi's core energy pulsed deep and strong, emanating waves of purple through his whole body system, and was deeply received by all of his other energy systems.

They shifted, expanded, and shuffled into more cohesion, letting go of the fears, the shame, the anger, and the pain. After a while, I became aware of a movement of energy towards Joshi. His energy systems were calling lost parts of him home again. This is usual when working deeply with the energetic core, and I see the same energy movement when working shamanically with soul retrieval. The feelings of loss, fear, trauma, and displacement all occur when there is a break in the wholeness of individual energy, and as his energetic core activated in its health and vitality, the wholeness returned. The 'lost boy' found his real home, deep inside himself.

From that point on, I have seen Joshi increasingly reclaiming his rightful place, not only within his corporate leadership work, but also in every part of his life. Since that day of healing and alignment, he has deeply anchored his sense of belonging in the world. Places where he avoided relationships or deep contact have become more accessible. He has started setting up his own business helping others connect deeply into their awakened soul purpose, and he continues to nurture his heart and soul closely, bringing his immense gifts into his daily life and into the world.

EXPERIENCING REAL CHOICE

In every aspect of your life, there are subconscious beliefs, thoughts, and understandings that, until you identify them and get curious about them, remain programmes that play out in your energy fields, repeating the validity of your truth again and again. This is not at all to say that the subconscious is a bad thing. Most of your body systems run on subconscious programming. But do you want your relationships to run on subconscious programming, playing out the same patterns you witnessed in relationships growing up, or trying desperately to be different from those patterns because they were too dysfunctional? Do you want to interact with your children, your partner, or your work colleagues out of habit? And maybe not even your own habits, but the subconscious habits that were programmed into your energy fields before you were seven years old?

The neuroscience and psychology are well understood. Until about seven years of age, a child's brain operates primarily in delta and then theta brainwave cycles. These are the same brainwave states that occur during hypnosis or meditation. At this point, your brain and energy systems are absorbing all the ways of being that are necessary for you, as part of the collective, to navigate through the amazingly complex functioning of being part of a human family, community, and society. In other words, your energy is laying down understandings about how to think about yourself, how to think about others, and how to interact with others. These energetic programmes shape your beliefs and values of what is right, what is wrong, what is you, and what is other. These are all essential parts of growing and are vital for you to navigate our complex human world.

The challenge comes when you believe that these understandings of the world represent a truth or even *the* truth. They don't. They represent your learning, your takeaways from the experiences of your life, which gradually develop into habits and ways of being. When you begin to believe something, that belief starts to run deeper and deeper through your energy and these 'programme glitches' play out in your energy fields. You aren't even aware of the way they are running the show, running your show, running your life.

How much of your day do you think you actively and consciously engage with? Take a guess. What percentage of your day are you on autopilot, being run by old programmes, and what percentage of your day are you actively and consciously engaging in your life?

Neuroscience research shows that most people are conscious between one percent and five percent of their day.[2] This means that what you actively and creatively engage in during your day is only one to five percent of it, and the rest is being run by the subconscious programmes held in your energy fields. This 99 to 95 percent of your day includes your

---

[2] Craig Gustafson, "Bruce Lipton, PhD: The Jump From Cell Culture to Consciousness," *Integrative Medicine* 16, no. 6 (December 2017): 44–50, PMID: 30936816; PMCID: PMC6438088, https://www.ncbi.nlm.nih.gov/pmc/articles/PMC6438088/; Simon Coghlen, "Controlling Your Subconscious Mind," Mount Merrion Physiotherapy, February 21, 2021, https://lorrainecarrollphysio.com.au/team-talk/how-to-control-your-subconscious-mind.html.

family time, your work time, your leisure time, your every time (apart from the one to five percent, which roughly translates to between 10 and 40 minutes of your day, spread over periods of just a few seconds at a time).

Now, don't groan, and if this stresses you out, then skip to page 291 and hold your stress repatterning points while you think about this mind-blowing statistic.

I also want to challenge that statistic. I feel that the huge shifts in consciousness that have been evolving within and around us over the last 10 years mean that our ability to engage in more everyday consciousness is steadily increasing. We are evolving and are becoming ever more conscious human beings.

There is a huge difference in your energy fields when you are engaging in conscious thought versus when you are not. When you are thinking consciously, even if it is only for a total of 30 minutes a day, your energy is organising around the creative field. When you are operating from the subconscious, your energy is organising around the habitual field. The difference between the two is mind-boggling.

To expand on what you learned in Chapter Two, your creative field is informed by your template of health. It is filled with the consciousness of potential and directly accesses the wisdom of your energetic core in all its personal and cosmic coding. You will most identify how your creative field feels in your system by recognising how you feel when you see something of immense beauty. Perhaps when watching a sunrise, you feel wowed and somehow a part of it. Maybe you are touched by it and slightly transformed because of it. That is your creative field activating in its fullness.

The habitual field is far more methodical. It can be cohesive and connective, and you can function wonderfully within it. You can laugh within it and play within it. It asks no questions of you. You don't have to explore the parts of you that you don't want to, and you don't have to 'work on' yourself. You can just tick along, exactly as you are, day after day. You can look at that sunrise and think, *Hey, that's gorgeous, isn't it?* and then move on through your day. When you exist in your habitual field, the point of connectivity between you and the energy around you loses its fluidity and relational creativity. You begin to close your worldview so that you are only able to resonate with what supports your thoughts and your programmed energy fields.

It would always delight me, truly to the depth of my soul, when a client would begin to engage their creative field in relation to their ailment. There would be a point for everyone when, as they talked about their illness or their life challenge, their habitual field would dissolve, as their creative field would explode into action and into view. I knew from that point on that they were walking, oftentimes leaping, towards health.

You may notice, though, that in my description of the habitual field, I wrote that it doesn't present you with any difficult questions to work out. And that is the lure and false security of the habitual field, of living from your subconscious. You can go through your day not having to take responsibility for yourself, what you say, what you think, or what you do. You can simply play out the programmes in your system and live in habit. You can blame your partner for causing that argument. You can blame your boss for being unfair. You can blame your parents for screwing you up, and you can blame the medical system for not being able to work out what is going on with you. And you can keep doing that every day, for decades, simply being a passive traveller within your own beautiful body.

The creative field doesn't let you get away with that.

Remember that definition of consciousness: your awareness of your own internal states, as well as the events going on around you. That means when you snap at your partner and react to what they say, resulting in you both engaging in a blazing row, you become aware (maybe later on, when you have cooled down!) that it was your reactivity that created the situation and take responsibility for it. You not only apologise to your partner, but commit to exploring what it was in your habitual energy field that got triggered, and you begin to heal that old programme. Once it is healed, you have access to more of your natural energy, your soul wisdom, and your engagement with your creative energy field.

That is hard work! And yet, energetically, the level at which you can engage in external connection depends entirely on the level at which you can engage in internal connection. The more you connect into yourself – your depths, your core, your inner world – the more attuned you will be to all that you are connected to externally (if there is such a thing as 'externally').

When you are able to engage more in your creative field, you will experience an increased expansion and contraction of all of your energy fields, like bellows fanning a fire, making it ever easier to live in that field. Like breathing, you breathe the external in and the internal out, continually engaging in and exchanging with the web of life. You are that connected.

AUTHENTIC BEING AND CONSCIOUS DOING

The power of breath is immense, for every minute of every day it represents continual exchange and connection. Your breath is relational and interconnective and houses the potential of balance in each full breath. A complete breath involves a complete turnaround of energy. You breathe in, which is an internal, yin activity. You breathe out, which is an external, yang activity. But what about in between the yin and the yang, the in and the out? At the top of your in-breath, you totally and utterly change direction – a volte-face that occurs 10 or more times a minute. At the bottom of your out-breath is exactly the same grand turning of direction. This continual switching between in and out, yin and yang, internal and external, holds the potential for bringing balance to all of your energy fields, and therefore all of your physicality.

An important consideration is that yin and yang are dynamic terms and are therefore relative to each other. So, for example, walking is a yang activity in relation to sitting still, but a yin activity in relation to going for a fast run. Nothing is an absolute or static yin or yang, but everything is an ongoing movement of flow between yin and yang. This is a fundamental principle of energy. In consciousness terms, the yin relates to your internal state, so we could refer to it as *being*, and the yang relates to your external state, so we could refer to it as *doing*.

This authentic being and conscious doing weave your energy fields together so you can move into more connective and conscious ways. You are moving towards 'unity consciousness,' which is where you are able to perceive your active role within the whole, rather than 'duality consciousness,' which is where you perceive yourself as separate and distinct from others.

When you engage in unity consciousness, you are working from the wisdom and energy of your energetic core. Your energetic core invites and inspires you to move in flow and alignment with the energy within and around us. This is the ease you experience when you are going with the flow, being present in the moment, while holding the vision and living or working in trust of a bigger cosmic pattern. This mindful soul connection allows you to fully embrace your essential place as a co-creator of not only your world, but the world in which we all live.

PRACTICES

Thinking:
Shining the Light of Your Focus

Think about what you would like to change about how you express yourself in your life. Are there places where you hold back from speaking your truth? Are there places and times when you restrict your own shining light, and if so, why? Think about how you would like to be able to express yourself, in every way, every day. Remember, your energy fields are fields of consciousness. When you focus your thoughts on the changes you would like to embrace in your life in order to be fully you, your energy can begin to coalesce around this intention.

Feeling:
Activate Your Template of Health

Let your mind wander around your understandings about your template of health. As you think about it, how do you feel? Take three nourishing breaths, feeling your body expanding and contracting. Can you feel your template of health pulsing with each fresh breath of life that you bring into your body? Slowly run your fingers across your skin; you are actually caressing your template of health. How does that feel?

Doing:
Writing the Book of Your Life

What will be written in your book of life? Give yourself at least 30 minutes to do this practice.

In this practice, you get to time travel in your mind. However old you are right now, jump along your timeline to when you are 97. You are at the stage of life of being deeply satisfied and content with everything your life has held, and you are getting ready to leave this physical life and die. From that perspective, look back at your long life and begin to write your own two-page obituary. Include your full name, who you are leaving behind, what kind of person you are, and what you have achieved in your life.

Attention is the rarest

and purest form of generosity.

~Simone Weil

(1908–1986)

YOU ARE
RESILIENT

Everyone has two choices.

We're either full of love

or full of fear.

~Albert Einstein

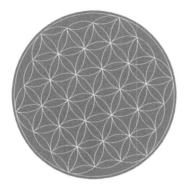

want you to feel safe, resilient, protected, and connected every minute of your day and night. Why? Because energetically, this is exactly how you are designed to feel so you can experience your fullest life, your big life, the most beautiful life you are here to live. If you don't feel like this is how you are currently experiencing your life, it means that parts of your energy fields aren't quite doing their job. Because when your energy fields are coherent, you are both protected and connected, and this means you are able to access a natural, easy resilience in all situations.

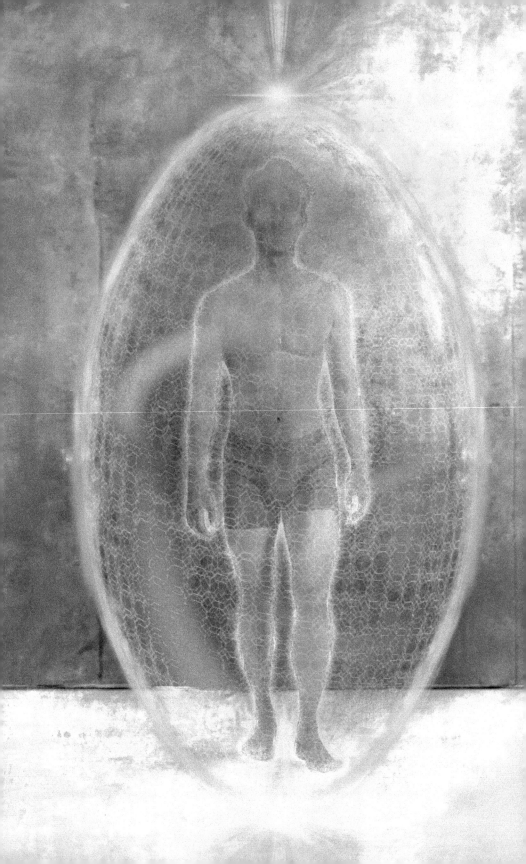

The *Oxford English Dictionary* defines resilience as, 'The quality or fact of being able to recover quickly or easily from, or resist being affected by, a misfortune, shock, illness, etc.; robustness; adaptability.'[1] All of that is true, yet feels quite meagre! Let's build on this definition:

- Resilience is being able to shine your own light into the world.

- Resilience is knowing you belong.

- Resilience is engaging in playful curiosity, opening doorways of potential inside yourself and inside your own life.

- Resilience is trusting the ground beneath your feet.

- Resilience is holding compassion and kindness for others, no matter what.

- Resilience is nurturing a growth mindset. Rather than saying, 'I can't do that' or 'I don't know that,' say, 'I can't do that *yet*' or 'I don't know that yet.'

←————————

When your energy fields are coherent, you are both protected and connected, and this means you are able to access a natural, easy resilience in all situations.

————————

[1]*Oxford English Dictionary*, 2nd ed. (Oxford: Oxford University Press, 2004), s.v. "resilience."

- Resilience is loving yourself and, in doing so, understanding how to love others despite the stumbles, falls, and outright crashes on the journey.

- Resilience holds you strong when pain knocks on your door.

- Resilience is birthed in tears when you sit with your pain and hug it close.

- Resilience is not ignoring the inner wounds that fester deep, but attending to and caring for yourself in the same way an animal licks its wounds to heal.

- Resilience is willingness to do the deep work, the shadow work, that would be so much easier to avoid.

You are only able to experience resilience in your daily life to the extent that your energy systems hold resilience. This level of 'energetic resilience' is a dynamic, fast, living process. It is the way your energy fields absorb something you are experiencing, such as an emotion, a memory, or a current situation, and flexes to meet and process that new energy before deciding what to integrate and what to reject.

Always remember that your energy fields are fields of consciousness. They are wise and aware and not something that is independent from 'you'. You are how you are because you *are* your energy systems, so your wisdom and consciousness are held in every part of your energy fields. When it comes to being energetically resilient, your energy fields are continually engaging in decision-making as they process the vast amount of information that surrounds you.

And not everyone is feeling resilient right now.

A COLLECTIVE CRISIS

Whether you look at the statistics for anxiety, depression, self-harm, or suicide, every mental health statistic is increasing each year, some steadily, some in startling leaps and bounds. Every one of those statistics speaks to the human story of an individual not being able to access their health or joy or experience the empowered and supported beauty of their unique and precious life. Every story is strikingly sad and cries the clarion call of the urgent need for more holism, more compassionate connection, and more collective healing within our societies.

Time after time in my clinic, I witnessed clients gradually realise that when it came to their own physical health, mental health, and overall vitality and engagement in life, they were powerful.

Really powerful.

In fact, they were the *only* person who could bring the healing needed for empowering themselves to take the leap forward they were so deeply seeking. In modern language use around health, it has become increasingly popular to describe the body as either 'healthy' or 'broken.' If 'broken,' the resultant step is usually to pick up the phone and make an appointment with a pharmacist or doctor to get whatever is needed to 'fix' you. This 'fix' is almost always chemical, in the form of a medication that will solve your 'brokenness.'

But the brokenness is not *you*. The reality is so much more complex and empowering. Whatever is showing up out of balance in your body is a symptom. I will say that again: anything physical that is presenting itself is a symptom. It is not the cause, and no matter what medication you use to treat the symptom, it is unlikely to ever heal the cause. This is because, by the time the imbalance has reached the point of showing up as a physical symptom, the root cause of that symptom is already being held deep within your energy systems. It is through healing that imbalance that the symptom can dissolve so you can once again experience your full health and vitality. You can learn how to understand, interpret, and nourish your energy so you are resilient in all situations.

When it comes to energetic resilience, a great visual to have is the continual process of the unfolding and enfolding of your energy fields, which is a continual flow from deep in your energetic core, out to the edge of your auric membrane (and sometimes beyond), and then back into your energetic core. For resilience, this entire process needs dynamic flex and flow. Depending on what your day brings, differing levels of expansion (unfolding) and contraction (enfolding) need to accommodate the multiple shifts in your thoughts, feelings, physicality, and situational experiences. Your energy fields will act differently when you are hanging out with friends, laughing and joking, versus when you are working with great focus on your next work project. When you have robust resilience, a broad range in the level of flex and flow occurs in your energy systems.

The challenge is when stress comes into your day, your life, and your energy fields. Stress is a crippling pandemic currently raging throughout the modern world. Stress changes everything about your energy fields and is the single reason resiliency can contract to the point of absence. When you meet your stress load – the breaking point of your resilience – you lose your ability to flex and flow and instead begin to track a fixed pathway filled with tension. Your creative field becomes stifled and your habitual reactive field kicks in. Within everyone's energy system is a point at which resilience stops being the natural programme and the wiring of defensive protection kicks in instead. At this point, there is no more expansion, no unfolding, and no flex, just tight, tense, narrow energy patterns of survival.

YOU ARE HERE TO THRIVE

Each one of your energy systems is involved with keeping you alive and allowing you to experience your most balanced and vital life. Each holds the balance between your ability to survive and your ability to thrive, a balance that is dynamic and changes with every thought you have or situation you find yourself in.

You are here not only to survive, but to *thrive*.

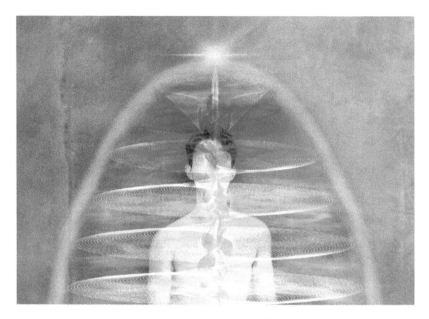

Each one of your energy systems is involved with keeping you alive and allowing you to experience your most balanced and vital life.

When you are in survival mode, you are living the most constricted existence you are capable of. Surviving is having to fight for your place. It is having to continually make an effort to be heard or respected. Surviving is that feeling you get some days when you wake up and the only thing you look forward to is being able to go back to bed at the end of the day. Surviving is stressful. Surviving is joyless.

The good news is that there is a lot you can do to help change your energy patterns from that of surviving to that of thriving. So let's explore what it feels like to thrive.

Thriving is living the most expansive existence you are capable of. It is that feeling that nothing is insurmountable, even if it is challenging. Thriving is seeing the magnificence in all of creation. Thriving is being able to burst out laughing with no hesitation. It is being able to live from your heart centre with trust and openness. Thriving is being able to say, 'I love myself. I love all of creation.'

Your energy is the first place you experience your world. When you know how to shift and manage your energy systems, you can quite literally change your life and how you experience it. You are extremely powerful, and you have 100 percent complete control over your personal world and worldview.

Your energy fields hold this understanding deep within their templates. Yes, you have an incredibly protective system that can take over most of the functioning of the physical and energetic when necessary, but remember you also have the template for optimum health and vitality that operates at every level of your energetic anatomy. It is this pattern of optimum health that you are able to encourage daily, and there are so many ways you can do this. One of the most wonderful and empowering aspects of understanding your energetic anatomy and the way it affects your physical body is that you really can affect deep and lasting change by consciously working with practices and simple techniques.

WEAVING YOUR PROTECTION

Every thought, every feeling, and every action has the potential to increase the flex and flow of your energy system. Being grounded, staying energetically cohesive, and being mindful of your thoughts, actions, and stress levels are all essential ways to nurture your resilience.

Every thought, every feeling, and every action has the potential to increase the flex and flow of your energy system.

As you learned in previous chapters, being grounded is essential; without this electromagnetic flow, your energy fields lose coherence and cohesion. Essentially, you begin to short-circuit yourself, and some areas of your energy fields start to collapse. Being grounded helps you stay in your power, and this means that when stress and difficulties are present in your life, you can meet them and still hold your own space, your own centre, your own sense of your magnificent self. At that point, your energy fields become deeply resilient.

Grounding means safety. When you are no longer electromagnetically grounded, your system knows you aren't safe, so your fight–flight–freeze stress response is easily triggered. This sets off a physiological cascade of hormones and chemicals that further impede your connective and balanced flow, and suddenly you are in a spiral of energetic reactivity.

It is this stress response that has the potential to limit your resilience. But stress isn't always a negative for you. In fact, depending on what it is, stress can even support the emergence of more natural resilience in your whole body system. Think of a time when you have had to meet and respond to a stressful situation and you managed it, felt the stress, and moved through it. This process helps lay down energetic patterns of resilience and neurological patterns of confidence in your ability to manage stressful situations.

Now think of a time when a stressful situation crippled you; when you responded by crashing into your most familiar fight–flight–freeze pattern. Did you fight, exploding in anger and excess defensiveness? Did you flee, leaving the situation, person, or deadline and cutting ties of connection in your attempt to leave the stress behind? Or did you freeze, paralysed by endless procrastination, and avoid the situation, blind or blinkered to the problem and pretending everything was OK?

All those strategies are wise and wonderful if your life is in danger. Truly. If a hungry grizzly bear has just busted through your door looking for the food in your kitchen, any one of the strategies of flight, fight, or freeze are highly effective. But very few stresses you engage with daily are life-threatening, and as such, you are called to evolve new and much more flexible strategies to manage them. These strategies need to encourage energetic, and therefore emotional, flex and flow. Effective stress management strategies encompass compassion and kindness towards yourself and others as well as conscious understanding of the situation. In meeting stress this way, you can maintain and nourish your resilience rather than be pulled into a chain of adrenaline-fuelled stress reactivity.

What I have observed over decades of watching the human energy system is that resilience is stretchy and elastic. Let's use the example of when a child attends a playgroup. That child has a lot to process. When a child feels stressed, they look for safety, perhaps moving closer to their parent as they assess the situation. As they process and begin to understand the situation, they explore where they can engage with the stress and venture closer to connect more with the previously stressful situation. Energetically, this relaxed and coherent movement throughout the child's energy system becomes much more still while the child is assessing stress. The wisdom held within their energy systems is scanning all its learned experiences to interpret safety or danger. When this process is nurtured in safety (as in moving closer to the parent), the child remains grounded and aware; they are engaging consciously with the process. From there, increasingly more movement comes back into their system, and leaps of radiance and expanding connectivity move in flashes of colour and bursts of electrical activity. As the child engages more and more with the situation that previously caused the big question mark of safety or stress, their system moves back into full flow and coherence.

However, what if there is no safety to process? What if the parent that child returned to for safety tells off the child, saying, 'Stop being silly. Go and play. You're always so frightened. There's nothing to be frightened about'?

When this happens, it can look like the child's energy system is in a state of internal paralysis; everything freezes, creating an inability for the child to process the situation. Stress is just heaped upon stress, and everything in the child's energy retreats, streamlining into the narrow pathway of protection and survival. There is no increase in resilience. Furthermore, it creates an energetic programme. Though still in its formative stage at that point, if this programme gets repeated again – the programme that 'new situations are not safe' and 'I am frightened and silly' – it becomes hardwired into the child's energy systems, leaving an energetic legacy for them to deal with as they progress through their life.

If you think of resilience as being elastic and stretchy, the objective is to nourish and aid that elasticity through self-care and conscious self-understanding. Knowing that you find meeting new people stressful because of an old glitchy programme in your energy fields means you can feel compassion for your stress and bring it back into harmony and health.

You can always get that flex, flow, balance, and joy back into your system; you can always heal your system because it is yours. In doing so, you create different ripples through your life, your family, your community, and the great web of life. These ripples are inspiring and empowering for all of us, for in our current ecological and social crisis, resilience is an essential prerequisite to every one of us living healthy, joyful, empowered lives.

Janie was mugged walking home from a get-together with friends. It was broad daylight. The assailant grabbed her bag, knocked her to the ground, and ran off. People came and helped her up, checked that she was OK, and stayed with her until she felt strong enough to continue her short walk home to her apartment in Bristol. Three months later, she walked into my clinic.

She explained that she had been a bright, happy, and confident student who was looking forward to her final exams and her future plans for travel and then work. But since 'that day,' her entire life had changed. She was frightened to go out on her own, she was scared even when she was with friends, she was struggling to get her college work done, and she had dropped out of the many clubs she had been part of for three years. She was jumpy in her apartment, had lost a lot of weight, and wasn't sleeping well. She also apologised for the way she sounded, for she had had a sore throat for weeks and her voice wasn't her usual one.

Looking at Janie's energy systems, I was unsurprised by what she was reporting and experiencing. As she was talking, many parts of her energy fields either ground to a halt, dissipated, or went into a kind of frantic, compensatory overdrive. The trauma of the event had knocked the cohesion and connectivity out of her energy systems and left her feeling in a place of free fall, with nowhere to land. She lost her sense of safety and belonging within the world. At that point, the world had become a hostile place for her to live within, and her fight–flight–freeze response had taken over the management of her body and gotten stuck.

What was also beautiful to see was the way in which her energy fields had not given up on attempting to restore balance by activating her template of health. Her chakras changed shape to try to accommodate gaps in her energy field, lemniscates leapt to connect areas and systems, her aura stretched, and her energy channels blipped and pulsed on and off as they tried to flow in the way they are designed to. The attempt was valiant, but it wasn't enough to initiate the movement and flow necessary for Janie's health to return or for her to access that deep sense of trust, joy, and vitality that is natural for everyone and had been her way of being before she was mugged.

Except for her energetic core where her energy was still beautiful, exquisite, and dynamic, Janie's energy fields just didn't know how to process the event and continue in its cohesive patterns. We worked together clinically, using energy and consciousness practices to invite the release of her imbalanced stress programmes, reconnect her patterns of health and vitality, and activate her template of health.

By the time Janie walked out of the room, her energy fields had recovered much of their natural vitality, and this immediately translated into her feeling more empowered, stable, and confident. She also noticed how much stronger her voice was, saying that she felt it was 'back to normal.' With practices to continue working with at home, Janie was able to maintain and increase her stability and confidence through the next few days before we were able to work again. It took three sessions for her to be able to 'return to herself' and have the energy and power to continue walking her own life path in her beautiful, joyful way.

The biggest challenge we needed to heal in Janie's system was not the actual assault or the fall to the ground, but her relationship of trust. This is the issue that broke her point of resilience. Until the day of the mugging, although she had experienced some heartbreak, Janie's life experiences had been secure and confidence-giving. She had great resilience to the ups and downs of her daily life. The mugging was the first time she had to personally face a different reality that there was also danger and fear, shock and injustice. This awareness had shaken her to her core and knocked her resilience into deep retreat. Not only was her sense of trust in the beauty and beneficence of life shaken, but this shake up was making her question her own trust in herself and her ability to navigate this new, expanded world. It was this issue of trust that we worked on together to return her natural vitality, energy, and power back into her day.

BUILDING RESILIENCE

How safe, resilient, and protected do you feel right now? What about when you go to the supermarket, spend time at hectic social gatherings, or come home from a long day of work and want to connect with your loved ones? Do you pick up on the energies that are around you? If you are with someone who is angry, do you feel affected and under attack? When you are in busy places, do you become sensitive to noise and lights, feeling wiped out by the time you get home and can regroup?

If you answered yes to any of these questions, you likely have a highly sensitive or empathic energy system that is tuned into everything around you, potentially leaving you drained, frazzled, and fractious.

Does this mean your sensitivity is a curse and you are always going to feel overwhelmed? That you have no choice? No! As someone who has a super-tuned, super-sensitive, super-plugged-in system, I am going to say that again: no, you do not need to be a victim of your own energetic sensitivity. Instead, you need to support your energy systems in slightly different ways than those who aren't particularly affected by what is around them.

Resilience is being able to shine your own light into the world.

Remember, energetic resilience is a dynamic, fast, living process; it isn't fixed. It is the way your energy fields absorb something such as an emotion, a memory, or current situation, and flexes to meet and process that new energy. There are four key areas of regular life where your energy systems need to hold resilience:

1. **Space Resilience**

   When you are in busy places such as supermarkets, social gatherings, crowds, or shopping centres with a lot of energy moving in multiple different ways, it can be a lot to process! There are people, artificial lights, noises, electric and electromagnetic pollutions, and geopathic stressors present, and your energy systems need to respond to all that external stimulus as well as whatever is going on in your own thoughts, feelings, and memories.

2. **Human Resilience**

You may find that when you are with other people, your energy dissipates. They may be people you love such as family members, people you work with, or total strangers that you pass on the street or sit beside while having your lunch. Your energy fields are connective; their energy fields are connective. That meeting point of connectivity may well be a beautiful, nourishing, and harmonious one, or it may be one that triggers you, pushes your buttons, and takes a high level of your resilience to maintain your grounded, easy balance.

3. **Immune Resilience**

Every minute of every day, you are surrounded by pathogens, such as bacteria and viruses, and your protective health systems need to be in good resilience so that these pathogens are either kept out of your energy and body or are quickly dealt with by your health system as soon as they show up. You rarely get colds, flus, or infections when you are feeling vibrant and energised. When you feel like that, the several layers of your protective energy systems are working in coherence to maintain your balance, health, and vitality. It is when there are already gaps in coherence and dips or holes in your resiliency (and therefore your protective energy systems) that those pathogens are able to breach your natural defences and settle into your body system.

4. **Collective Consciousness Resilience**

At the moment, the collective consciousness field is asking for an evolutionary leap, and many people are feeling the effect of the out-of-balance manner in which human society is progressing in the mainstream. This may show up as world grief or an underlying feeling of fear and anxiety, despite the fact that there is nothing in your life pointing you towards those emotions. Your experiencing of these pressures are your wisdom systems calling for your awareness, and if you aren't able to hold your resilience, the burden can be overwhelming. How do you feel when you watch the news? Or a wildlife documentary that illustrates the desperate plight of so many in the animal world? Just thinking about it can create feelings of grief, weariness, disempowerment, and hopelessness, and these feelings in turn immediately affect your energy fields, creating a dip or crash in their vitality and coherence.

In my practice and teaching is a belief I have come across quite a bit: you can't be open, aware, intuitive, and connected *and* be protected at the same time. I suggest this is a myth, and a damaging one at that, for everything about the way your energy systems work testifies differently.

In the amazingly intricate and complex energy anatomy that is you, connection means protection, and protection means connection.

Protection does not mean

- Your shields go up and nothing can penetrate.

- Your intuition is blocked.

- You have limited empathy or compassion.

- You will miss out on anything in your life that enhances you and your ability to be your fullest self.

When you activate your energy systems in their balance and health, then your fullest, most magnificent protection kicks in.

Protection does mean

- Not having to react in a fight–flight–freeze response in situations that aren't life-threatening.

- Not being influenced by the energies around you to the extent that you become knocked off your own balance as you walk your unique life path.

- Not allowing excess electromagnetic influence (e-smog) to reside in your energy field.

- Being able to stay grounded in all situations.

- Enabling your system to be resilient so that it can both expand and contract in balance.

- Easing your ability to connect and relate with others in your life.

- Allowing your energy to be in service of your full expression and becoming rather than working super hard to clear energetic toxicity.

- Not experiencing overwhelm.

- Having the ability to always feel safe.

Built into your energy fields is a continual awareness of what is you and what is not you, meaning that you are both totally unique *and* connected to every energy field around you. From the depth of your energetic core to the edge of your aura, your energy fields are continually unfolding away from your centre and enfolding back into your centre, exchanging information as this happens in order to help you find your complete expression in this world, keep you safe, and aid your process of becoming. When you work to support your energy, you are able to support your physical health, your emotional health, and your vitality. You can support your groundedness so that it remains even when you are in stressful or sensitive situations. You are hardwired for resilience, health, joy, and empowerment.

PRACTICES

Thinking:
Concentric Circles of Connection

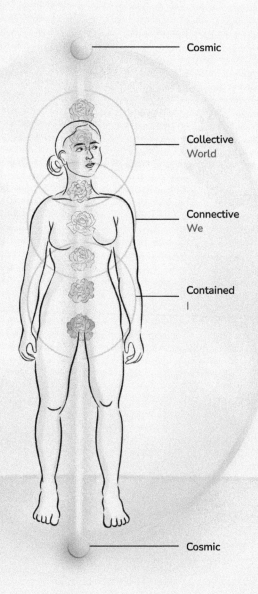

Cosmic

Collective
World

Connective
We

Contained
I

Cosmic

Have you ever really thought about how deeply you are connected to all of life? To enhance your resilience, it can be profoundly informing and inspiring to consciously identify the levels of connection you are currently experiencing in your life. The levels you will be exploring are those of the collective, the personal, and the sacred.

You may get extra energetic benefit by turning these thoughts into action and writing a list of the following:

1. Think about and write down how you are connected to people. This may be your family, friends, work colleagues, neighbours, and so on. Think about those closest to you, then expand into your broader community, and even the global community that the internet has made possible.

2. Think about and write down how you are connected to yourself. What do you do to nurture self-exploration, self-compassion, self-reflection, and self-awareness?

3. Think about and write down how you are connected to the sacred – the great web of life you live within. What do you do to nurture your relationship with the natural world? The cosmic world? How do you connect to your ancestors and support the world that is being created for your descendants?

Feeling:
Activating the Stress Repatterning Points

In the middle of your forehead, above both your eyes, there are two amazing points of energy called 'stress repatterning points.' Have you ever stood on the bank of a lake and looked down into deep water? On one level, there is a vast stillness to the water, and on another level, there is deep, rich movement. That is exactly what the energy of these points on your forehead looks like. When you are stressed, the rich, deep dynamism becomes less apparent on the surface, and (to continue the lake metaphor) it can seem as if a thin layer of ice has formed. Whether they realise it or not, all humans know the power of these points. How often have you put your hand on your forehead when you are stressed, shocked, alarmed, disheartened, or in despair? Children do it. Adults do it. We see people do it in films and instinctively on the news (and it is a great thing for you to do while *watching* the news!). By gently covering these stress repatterning points with your palm or fingers, you can 'unfreeze' the energetic stagnation caused by whatever stress you are experiencing or reliving. The benefits of these points don't stop there, however, for once they have 'unfrozen,' continuing to hold them initiates a flow of energy from the surface of the point to deep within many of your energy systems. This means that you can bring greater and greater release to the root cause of the stress pattern within your energy, changing your stress response and bringing you more space, flow, and resilience.

Your stress repatterning points.

1. Get really comfortable and set yourself up so you can place either the palm of your hand or hands over both stress repatterning points. If you are lying down, you may want to put pillows under your arms to support their weight. If you are sitting, then have your elbows resting on your legs, a table, or the arms of a chair. Be careful not to put a lot of pressure on the points you are holding. The energy needs to flow through these points, so you want to maintain a gentle pressure on them to allow this flow.

2. Cover your two stress repatterning points using either one hand or both. It will depend on how you can be most comfortable and whether you are sitting or lying down.

3. Take three nourishing breaths to begin the reset.

4. If you are doing this practice for restorative reasons to help create more flex and flow within your whole body system, simply hold your stress repatterning points for several minutes; or if in bed, until you fall asleep!

5. If you are consciously bringing attention to a current or previous stress experience, think about the experience as you hold your stress repatterning points. It may be helpful for you to speak your thoughts aloud to yourself as you hold the points. Language provides an active energetic bridge between the conscious and the subconscious, making this practice even more effective.

6. Continue to hold, talk, and think until you feel that there has been a reduction in the charge around the stress or issue.

7. Remember that stress patterns are often held in many layers, so it may be useful to come back to this process a few times to bring deeper and deeper harmony to the relevant stress response.[2]

 Doing:
Wings of Strength

This is my favourite practice to aid the elasticity and flexibility of your energy systems and nurture your biggest resilience.

1. Bring your hands together in front of your chest with your thumbs gently pressing into your breastbone.

2. Breathe in deeply as you visualise that the oxygen and fresh energy you are bringing into your body are stoking up your battery one breath at a time.

3. As you breathe out, visualise that you are holding all that fresh oxygen and energy deep inside you.

4. Do this for at least three breaths.

---

[2] With loving thanks to *Touch for Health Kinesiology*, and my teacher and energy medicine pioneer Donna Eden, for deepening my understanding of the stress repatterning points.

5. When you feel ready, bring in an energising breath, and this time, as you breathe out, move your hands out, palms first, as far as your arms can stretch. It doesn't matter which direction you move your arms. You are moving them out to the edge of your own aura, and as you do, the energy that you have been building inside you will be moving through your hands so that your aura becomes more and more energised. It is as if your arms are wings that are building the strength all around you.

6. Keep repeating this breath and your arm and hand movement until you feel strong, safe, and resilient.

Remember, I have created videos of many of the practices in this book, so I can guide you as we do them together. You can find these videos and other supporting material at www. pruneharris.com/radiant-soul.

Truth does not change because it is, or is not, believed by a majority of the people.

~Hypatia of Alexandra

(351–415)

13

THE GIFT OF
BELONGING

The most important decision we make is whether we believe we live in a friendly or hostile universe.

~Albert Einstein

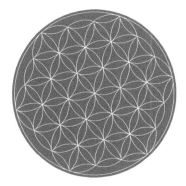

Every day, you receive more gifts than are possible to count:

- The gift of the ground beneath your feet.

- The gift of the air you breathe.

- The gift of the water that you drink.

- The gift of life.

You are given these gifts—not because you have a human right to them or have worked to earn them. You are given these gifts because you and your precious life are part of something much greater.

No matter where you are living, how you are feeling, or what you are doing or not doing with your life, you already belong. You do not have to fight to secure your place in this

web of life, or to protect it. The gift of belonging was given to you at birth.

Do you have a memory of knowing that you belong? That deep sense of certainty of place, acceptance, and connection where you feel safe and welcome? Perhaps it was as you were held in the arms of your mum or dad, sat around a table at a family dinner, or spent time with your special friends at school. When you experience that feeling of belonging, your energy fields respond. Your system grounds more, deactivating your fight–flight–freeze response as the energy of safety moves throughout your whole body. Your heartfield lights up, and from it radiates the song of the soul. All of this means that your habitual energy field loosens up, and you are able to engage more consciously so you can create space in your system, space in your relationships, and creative responsive space within the community that has helped engender that sense of belonging.

And when did you start feeling that you didn't belong? When was it that this deepest understanding that is always running through your core, claiming your place as an essential part of life on Earth, got rocked, shaken up, and possibly disintegrated?

Energetically, you are created by the Cosmos, and in turn, you create the Cosmos. Each vibration that you put into that great web of life affects and influences the vibration of the

← ⎯⎯⎯⎯⎯⎯⎯⎯

You and your precious life are part of something much greater.

whole, which in turn, affects you. The unfolding and enfolding principle of your human energy fields is at play in every part of life with the simultaneous and continual exchange of energy flowing both ways. This is something that was deeply understood in Indigenous communities, including your own ancient indigeneity, for every culture, every people, every race, and every ethnicity has indigeneity at its roots.

What you think of as coincidence or synchronicity is actually energy exchange, and even in your own life over the past month, I am sure the examples of 'coincidence' are endless. How about you don't see them as coincidences anymore, but as examples of how interrelated and interconnected you are at every level?

After reading the chapter about your energetic core, you know that at the very centre of your energy system is a flow of energy that is both essentially yours and connects you to all of creation. From your core, this soul vibration emanates through your whole body system, your physical body, your energy fields, and your thought fields. It flows through every part of your being, every part of you.

Remember, you can think of your energetic core as a superhighway of information and sacred energy. It is through this superhighway that you connect all that is above and all that is below you, as well as all the energies associated with

Your energetic core empowers you to be a living link between the Earth and the Cosmos. You are essential.

these two very different vibrations. When you go for a walk on the beach and feel infinitely better afterwards, it means the flow of energy through your energetic core has been activated and grounded – grounded down into Earth consciousness and grounded up into cosmic consciousness. You feel balanced, more at peace, healthier, and better able to connect into the depth of your being; and from that place, you are better able to connect to other people or other beings. Your sense of belonging expands towards your natural birthright. What happened to shake that up for you?

This gift of life isn't a one-way flow with you passively receiving the air, the water, and the ground beneath your feet, for you are in continual exchange with the Cosmos. When you breathe air, you bring it into your body, use it for your health and balance, and then breathe it back out for the rest of nature to use differently. You return it to the whole. When you drink water, you bring it into your body, use it for your balance, and then return it to the essential water cycle of this planet for it to be used again and again and again; you return it to the whole. When you are born, you engage in the gift of your life until your death, and then you return that gift of life to the whole.

What will it take for you to reclaim your gift of belonging? Because it is yours. And it is never too late to take it back. You are an essential part of a cosmic miracle that is continually unfolding, and nowhere is that more apparent than in your energy fields, for they connect you into everything that is around you at all moments of every day and night. Whether you are sharing with others a house, a bedroom, a bed, a village, a town, a city, or the planet, everyone's energy fields are in constant connection and communication with one another. This is because you are an essential living organism within the greater living organism of this planet, which in turn, is a living organism within the greater living organism of the Cosmos.

And all of it is connected energetically through the great web of life, with each thread an essential part of the whole. You are an essential part of that whole, and being able to embrace this understanding is the single biggest determinant of *everything* about your energy fields and therefore your thoughts, your emotions, your actions, and your life. The gift of belonging is the greatest gift, and it is yours to accept at any moment you choose.

If we went for a walk through the woods together, I would see your energy fields shift and change as they came into relationship with the trees we were walking through. Not only that, but our energy fields would change depending on what kind of tree we were walking, standing, or sitting beside. Hawthorn particularly affects the heartfield, oak affects the stomach meridian, linden lightens the aura, beech encourages strong movement of the human energy fields down towards the Earth, and birch encourages showers of movement through the aura. All of them affect your electrical system and therefore your heart energy. And meanwhile, your energy affects the energy field of the tree you are in an energetic relationship with. This is true for all parts of the natural and elemental world, whether it is trees, plants, flowers, stones, water, or any other part of nature. It is true of the land itself, for your energy fields are in continual relationship with the patch of Earth that you live upon.

In my energy fields is the presence of a deep, green vibration that is constant, but not quite mine. It is the vibration of the hills of Cornwall, and it vibrates in a way that sings to my soul every day. It exists within my energy, even when I am far from Cornwall. It is the energy of the land that grew me and is a vibrational hue that helped shape me in every way. This will be true for you too, and the energy of where you grew up and where you live now will continually and subtly influence your energy fields.

Stepping into your empowered relationship as co-creator of your life – and therefore co-creator of the web of life – is a great awakening, and it is happening person by person, community by community.

Jenny presented in my clinic asking for help with her lower back and hips. She was living in chronic pain and felt like she had a vice on this part of her body. She had always been an active woman who loved sports, hiking, and gardening, but her physical pain was robbing her of being able to engage in any activity, making her feel isolated and frustrated. This had gone on for almost two years, and her pain was resistant to all the biomedical and holistic health modalities she had engaged in. She found that whatever she tried would work for a few days, but then the pain would return and she would be back to square one. She was also lonely, as many of her social activities involved being active. Jenny had lost her social network as well as her physical health.

As I looked at her energy systems, many things became apparent. Firstly, she was incredibly strong. Her willpower and determination shone from her core through every cell, illustrating that she was deeply connected to herself and to the song of her soul. I knew if we could find the essential imbalance in her system, her healing would be fast and complete.

Every time I looked at the area where Jenny was experiencing pain, I saw the entire energy field at the back of her body collapse in on itself. Her aura dissolved, her chakras dropped, and everything became unstable. In the attempt to restore and rebalance her whole body system, energy shot from her lower chakra but crashed around in her lower back and hip area, unable to find its way into connection. No wonder she was feeling such pain!

The next important understanding was that, even when all this pain and instability occurred, her big protective system did not engage in fight–flight–freeze. That was pretty remarkable, bringing me back to Jenny's immense strength.

So what was going on?

At times like this, I start playing energy detective, looking for clues. With her permission, I stood behind

Jenny while we chatted. I wanted to watch how her energy responded to our conversation. When she talked about her dependent husband, I saw the sadness in her second chakra, but that didn't engage the collapse of the energy field behind her. When she talked about missing her friends, I watched as the energy in her throat constricted in grief and her liver organ flared with the emotion of frustration, but that, too, didn't engage the collapse of the energy field behind her.

Then Jenny talked about how much she missed being able to go for a walk, as she loved taking long walks on her own. When she was a child, she grew up on the Norfolk Broads and would walk for hours every day. She expressed that she loved that area and asked if I had ever been. I almost cried with the emotion that exploded through her energy – a longing so deep, a beloved so missed. And now I could see what was happening.

Her aura didn't disappear in a violent and rapid movement; it got sucked into her lower back in a powerful place on her spine in line with her waist. At that point is a portal into the lower dantian and the energetic core, and it was holding such a deep imbalance that it was knocking off her entire energy system and creating pain in her hips and back.

I then knew what else to look for. In every person's energy system is an ancestral vibration. It is the sum of the family field you are a part of, for without every single one of your ancestors, you simply wouldn't exist. That family field can hold the energy of balance or of imbalance, and Jenny's was rocking, shifting, flaring, and then collapsing. For Jenny to heal, it needed balancing; it needed healing.

In that first session, as I was working to relieve the pain in her body and reconnect her auric field and chakras, we talked about her family. She was the first person in many generations to leave Norfolk. Her parents were dead, and although she had no siblings, she still had many cousins and other family members living in or close to the Norfolk Broads. When I asked her when she had last been home, she said, 'Oh, that isn't home anymore. I haven't been there for 12 years, since Mum died.'

A strange vibration started moving through her energy fields just then, like a low song or note. These were her nadis, her songlines, which resonate with sound as they activate, and it was happening now in Jenny's system. To me, it sounded like a calling from deep within her soul, and I suspected it held the key to her pain. Explaining what I had perceived in her energy fields, I suggested that she visit her homeland. I went a step further and proposed that, rather than just taking a 'holiday,' she intend it as a healing pilgrimage to that land to honour her ancestors, reconnect with her physical and human family, and reconnect with the land and water of the Norfolk Broads.

Within a month, Jenny had done just that. It was a profound experience for her as she reconnected with her childhood places, placed flowers on the graves of her passed family members, reconnected with cousins, and spent time with someone who was tracing their ancestry while stories were shared and discovered. They were stories of her youth, her parents, her family animals, the regular flooding, the isolation within the community, and the traditions either stuck to doggedly or rejected. Each story wrapped her more strongly in reconnection and healing. She spent 11 days in Norfolk reconnecting, and on the fifth day, she realised she had walked for two hours and felt no pain. By the 11th day, she was walking, swimming, and laughing again, with no pain.

When Jenny returned to her husband and her home, she was able to re-engage with her usual life and all of her activities. We worked together on and off for a few years as she explored even more layers of ancestral healing and deep reconnection, and she never experienced that pain again. And yes, she returned to Norfolk regularly, reclaiming it as hers and thriving within that reconnection and deep knowledge of belonging.

WHAT STOPS YOU FROM FULLY EMBRACING THE GIFT OF BELONGING?

Do you feel like you belong simply because you are alive? So often, a sense of belonging comes from a sense of being accepted by others. When you are accepted by your family, a group, or your 'tribe,' you have a sense of belonging. Can you expand that to a global perspective and perceive that you are accepted because you belong to this web of life? And you *do* belong in this web of life because you are a part of it and therefore are accepted unconditionally.

In a world where the story of separation and reductionism is our cultural norm, this understanding of interconnectiveness can be such a difficult one to get your head around. You are never separate. You may be on your own or sitting in sacred solitude, but you are still connected at every level of your being.

To unpack this for a moment, let's have a look at one of the most damaging myths of our modern culture: survival of the fittest. This myth's central theme is the understanding that only the strongest will survive and achieve success and that they do so at the cost of others, as well as at the cost of their deep connection to themselves and the calling of their soul.

More accurately, the natural world holds that everything has its place in the intricate design of creation, and no place is more important than the other. Even those who live in hierarchical societies, such as baboons or wolves, understand that the hierarchy only exists because of the interdependence between and among every individual. It is not about mastery, but about interdependence. The overarching structure in nature is cooperation and mutual symbiosis. Whether you look at ants, elephants, a pride of lions, or emperor penguins, you will see a focus on the collective.

Survival of the fittest is gradually becoming recognised as simply inaccurate. 'Tend and befriend' is a much more common strategy in nature and the human world, and it is not only in your own energy fields but in your physical body, too.

For 'you' are not a single entity. You never can be.

Do you know that there are more non-human cells in your body than there are human cells? The most recent research suggests that only 43 percent of the cells in your body are human, and the rest are bacteria, fungi, viruses, and archaea.[1] You are an amazing symbiotic organism, and for you to be healthy, you are entirely reliant on the interdependence of all.

In your gut alone, there are over four pounds of healthy bacteria that are essential for your well-being. In fact, when you understand there is more non-you DNA than you DNA, it creates the question of who you are.

Are you an individual, or are you a symbiotic organism?

If we think of Planet Earth as a grand organism teeming with other organisms, perhaps each of us is a miniature representation of the planet. If you didn't have the good bacteria in your gut system, then not only your digestion but

---

[1] James Gallagher, "More Than Half Your Body Is Not Human," BBC News, April 10, 2018, https://www.bbc.com/news/health-43674270.

your immune system, your vitality, and your very life force would be severely compromised. So you need that bacteria just as much as it needs you. You are a symbiotic organism, not an individual.

It is time to throw out the concept that only the fittest survive. It is incorrect and always was, although it perfectly suited the worldview of the mainstream culture that created it in the 19th century. In our evolving human world, the story of survival of the fittest is a poor story to be building our societal worldview around; it rests on the premise that we can only thrive at the expense of others, minimises the worth of compassion and kindness, and undermines our community and sense of connection. If we plug ourselves into the belief of this myth, we narrow the world's mentality into believing that the world is a hostile place where 'dog eat dog' rules apply and the world divides into 'have and have-nots.' It engenders the extremes of either dominant aggression or scarcity mentality.

'Dog eat dog!' Even writing it, it seems like such a daft statement. Anyone who has ever lived with dogs and seen them raise their puppies, play together, live together, lick and warm the wounded, and grieve their dead will shake their head at the deep inaccuracy of this statement. Yes, there are fighting dogs and they will kill each other, but only when humans have raised them to do so, often in extreme cruelty. That is not the natural way a dog lives, yet we have taken the assumption of survival of the fittest and the concept of 'dog eat dog' deep into our collective psyche. Our energy fields and this deep programming can spill over into so many parts of daily life, for the legacy of survival of the fittest remains an unexplored belief and damaging assumption. It has slotted into our habitual energy fields and just keeps playing out.

How many of our assumptions are unexplored and unexamined, yet rule so much of our subconscious thoughts? What about 'fighting like cats and dogs' and the old premise that dogs and cats can't coexist in harmony? You probably know of a personal example in which a cat and dog live together in peace, and I want to share two stories of the deep bond that animals can create with each other despite our human beliefs or assumptions!

I have already mentioned the dog that came into my life when I was eight years old and that my mum brought home two kittens to help me while I was ill in bed in my teenage years. My dog came into milk and nursed those two kittens. Their claws shredded her skin as they pawed while they drank, and she would bleed every time, yet she would still present her teats to those little kittens every day.

My family and I have had cats and dogs in our life for many years now. One winter, we went away for two weeks to visit family in Canada. Our dog, Luna, went down the road to stay with my dad, and a neighbour fed our very independent cat, Max. When we arrived home from our holiday, Max promptly arrived home to greet us. He had a huge welt on his head that must have happened soon after we had left, because it was infected, filled with pus, and smelt horrendous. Luna worked for 40 minutes to lick the wound clean, and Max simply lay there until it was done. Every day, and several times a day for the first few days afterwards, Luna would clean the wound until it healed.

None of these (much beloved) animals questioned whether they 'should' act in the way they did. They didn't know they were breaking societal norms of pre-existing and unexplored assumptions. They responded in wholeness and connectivity.

Recently, I was interviewed live on a social media channel. I love the exchange of being interviewed and was enjoying the dynamic questions of the interviewer. Halfway through, she asked my opinion of something she had recently been told and was giving serious consideration to. 'In life', she said, 'there are people who have been beaten down and there are people who are going to become beaten down. So why should we believe that things are going to get better? Why shouldn't we believe that we've finally found the truth that life is a struggle and horrible and we're going to die and so on?' I was stopped in my tracks. I felt the shock waves move through my energy fields as I was reminded that this disheartened, hopeless belief is guiding the daily life of many people, corporations, and institutions. This is the shocking and saddening legacy of the story of separation and survival of the fittest: the story encourages separation from self and from the deepest parts of our energy fields. The story of our energy is one of connection, not separation – connection to self, connection to others, and connection to the Cosmos.

FROM PHYSICAL CELL TO COSMIC CELL AND BACK AGAIN

For a moment, see yourself as a single cell out of the 30 trillion plus cells in your beautiful body. You are complete and contained within your cell membrane. To be a healthy cell, you need nutrition, a digestive system, a respiratory system, and an elimination system. You have an important job to do as part of the human body system, and you connect with the community of cells around you to do it. What is your important job? Being a co-creative part of the human that is you.

Next, see yourself as a single human being out of the over seven billion human beings on our beautiful Earth. Oh, you really are! You are complete and contained within your auric membrane. Just like every cell in your body, you need nutrition, a digestive system, a respiratory system, and an elimination system to be a healthy human. You have an important job to do as part of the human species, and you connect with the community of humans around you to do it. What is your important job? Being a co-creative part of the human species.

Now, see the human species as one out of the billions of species living together on Earth. Each species is complete and contained within its unique energy field. Each species needs nutrition, a digestive system, a respiratory system, and an

———————→

You are the individual cell and the individual human. You are also the collective human playing an essential part in co-creating the Cosmos.

elimination system. Each has an important job to do as part of life on Earth, and each connects with the community of species around to do it. What is the job of each species? Being a co-creative part of the Cosmos.

You are the individual cell *and* the individual human. You are also the collective human playing an essential part in co-creating the Cosmos. Whether you explore quantum mechanics, traditional shamanic cosmology, or the organising principle of any field of energy, you exist energetically on many levels at any one time. The easy truth is that you are a whole and intact individual, a part of a larger family unit that is whole and intact, *and* a part of a greater community. This greater community may include animals, land, trees, plants, and rivers. You are in a continual energy exchange with all that is around and within you, a magnificent symbiotic relationship with all of life. Every thought, emotion, action, or inaction creates a vibration, a wave of energy through the cosmic field, in just the same way that ripples move across a still lake when you drop a pebble in.

Right now, over seven billion humans are creating waves of energy through the web of life. And depending on what each person is thinking, feeling, doing, or not doing, the vibrations are different. Some of those vibrations will positively reinforce me, you, and us, and others will challenge you, me, and us. Each one shapes you just as the energy of your thoughts, emotions, actions, and inactions shape them. You affect everything; everything affects you. Which means you can never feel a victim of your own life, your own glitchy programming, other people, or anything else. Realise that you are essential; you are connective; you are a co-creator of your world, and you always, always belong. You are not only an awesome human being, but an awesome cosmic being.

So here we are, together, creating a new story and a new reality. Life is not about fighting for survival. Survival should rarely have to be what we are hoping to achieve. Survival is about protection and living your smallest life, while thriving is creative growth that brings about creating, discovering, and engaging in your fullness.

Right now, as you are reading this book, there are millions if not billions of people who engage every day with trust, compassion, kindness, and connection. We are seeing phenomenal movement within social, business, political, and justice systems where more people are looking around and questioning just what the bottom line justifies. Collective consciousness is growing by the breath as more people reach for a future that is sustainable, nourishing, and balanced. A future where you already know you belong because you are part of its creation.

PRACTICES

Thinking:
Your Own Sense of Belonging

Think about how much you feel that you belong, and now rate it. Use a scale of 0–10, with 0 meaning, 'I don't feel I belong at all. I don't even trust the ground beneath my feet' and 10 meaning, 'I feel this in every part of my being. I know I belong as an active and co-creative part of this vast universe.'

Feeling:
The Ground Beneath Your Feet

This will take 10 or more minutes.

1. Find a place outside where you can stand or sit that is within 100 metres of where you live. It may be in your garden or at a bench close to your apartment. Be comfortable whether you are sitting or standing.

2. Take a moment to think about and feel into all the stories that this piece of ground has been witness to – all the history, movement, and change. This ground existed before humans did.

3. Take some nourishing breaths and allow your awareness to sink towards your centre, your core.

4. Feel into the ground beneath your feet. Visualise, think, feel, and imagine that there is energy flowing from your feet into the ground.

5. Visualise, think, feel, and imagine nourishing energy from the Earth coming through your feet, through your aura, and into your whole body system.

6. Feel gratitude for the ancient wisdom of this land you are on. Share that gratitude through your energy fields, thanking the land that supports you.

Doing:
Earth Electrics

We have all the science to understand that we absorb essential, life-giving energy from the Earth. With only a little time and some soil, it is possible to tap into the electrics of the Earth and get an electric treatment more organically powerful and healing than any practitioner or machine can give us. Working with the Earth's electrics is an amazing way to help transform our energy systems.

I have taught about the Earth's electrics to many students who love to experience the deep, revitalising healing they provide. It can be done in your garden, a park, a field, or anywhere you can sit or lie with your fingers in the soil. And it really is that simple.

1. Enhance your energy to get the most out of working with the Earth's electrics by massaging your hands and feet before you start, which readies them to help move the flow of energy through you unimpeded.

2. Sit or lie on the ground outside in a position that you can easily hold for five minutes or more.

3. Once you are comfy, bury your fingertips in the ground so that the earth is covering your fingernails. Sometimes the connection is established within a minute or so, other times it takes several minutes, but hold the position for as long as you have available to you.

4. Relax and enjoy the gift of the Earth's electrics moving through your body. Some people experience excess energy or tension moving out of their body, others feel energy moving into their system, and some experience both of these energetic directions. All of these experiences leave them relaxed and recharged.

I have seen powerful and profound changes occur in people who work with this practice regularly, not only in their health and vitality, but also in their connection to themselves, others, and all of creation.

Remember, I have created videos of many of the practices in this book, so I can guide you as we do them together. You can find these videos and other supporting material at www.pruneharris.com/radiant-soul.

"Hope" is the thing with feathers

that perches in the soul

and sings the tune without words

and never stops – at all.

~Emily Dickinson

(1830–1886)

14

How Kind
Can You Be?

Compassionate people are geniuses in the art of living, more necessary to the dignity, security, and joy of humanity than the discoverers of knowledge.

~Albert Einstein

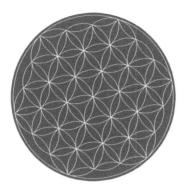

E nergetically, every time you are kind, your heart becomes the portal for wholeness and for completion of your soul's desire for expression. In this way, kindness, compassion, and gratitude are all gateways to experiencing the mystery of the universe.

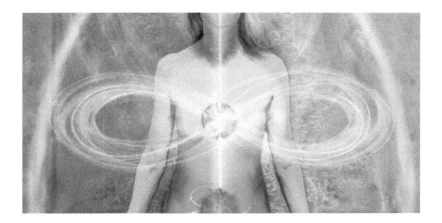

There is so much to say about the energy of kindness, and it is a delight to write about. It may be no surprise to you that anytime you feel kindness, compassion, or gratitude, your energy fields expand. What immediately becomes apparent to me when watching the energy of kindness is that there is no such thing as a 'small' act of kindness; every act of kindness is mighty in its reverberations, and there can be no quantifying measure of it. An act of kindness has the same value, whether it is a smile to a stranger or a five million dollar donation to a charity. Thinking of kindness as measurable is trying to fit it into a scale of worth in which the energy of kindness has no place, for kindness is always more powerful than any possible system we could use to measure it.

Kindness creates an energetic response throughout your whole body system. If I were trying to describe what happens in terms of 'first this happens, then that happens,' it would go something like this:

- First, your lower dantian activates in your energetic core.

- Then, your second chakra glows, activating the root chakra and the heart chakra, too.

- Then, your heartfield lifts.

- Then, you are more grounded up and down, in and out.

- Then, all of your dantians activate and radiant core energy emanates through every cell.

- Then, your electric system sparks brighter and deeper.

- Then, your aura rockets with strength and light.

- Then, you smile, and all that light pours out of your eyes.

But all of that is nonsense, for it all happens simultaneously as soon as you and kindness meet each other and your template of health sings its song of joy, connection, and existence.

Can you imagine that? An instantaneous transformation that affects every part of your physical, emotional, cognitive, and energetic body? It is *amazing*! And it is totally, totally normal. This is what your energy system is designed to convey throughout your body, your thoughts, your actions, and your life. Kindness is your natural way of being, and anything that impedes that natural and immense kindness limits you – and by this, I mean the *real* you, the *deep* you, the *authentic* you.

Kindness is like a switch in your system. It is either on or off. Can you imagine what society would be like if everyone's kindness switch was on? Can you imagine what it will be like when it *is* and you have been a part of creating that reality?

When you receive kindness, every part of your energy anatomy is enveloped by it. When you are kind to another, every part of your energy anatomy is activated by it. And when you are kind to yourself, every part of your energy anatomy receives nourishment. Kindness also changes your physical life.

It can heal digestive, reproductive, hormonal, and physical issues. Kindness connects, and in doing so, changes your life.

One of the other amazing things about kindness is that it is highly contagious. Kindness engenders kindness. An energy field that has its kindness switch on helps turn it on in everyone else around it. When you are touched by the kindness of another, what happens in your energy system is exactly what I described above and more, for this is where gratitude and compassion step in as well.

The energies of gratitude, compassion, and kindness have a lot in common, but there are subtle differences. Compassion is deeper; its vibration is an expression of your core energy, your soul energy. The energy of soul joy and soul compassion are the same, and from this deep root flows the energy of kindness and gratitude. Does that make sense? Compassion and joy are innate in you, and they create the kindness and gratitude that you extend to yourself and others. Compassion exists in your deepest energy systems; kindness and gratitude are the result of it.

At about the time we moved into this new millennium, I started noticing a different vibration in many of the children being born. It had a transparent, luminous quality I had hardly ever seen in the soul colour of people up to that time. My daughter, born in 2003, had this energy, and there were increasingly more children being born around this time who had it, too. Because each human being is a cosmic being and part of the co-creation of the Cosmos, just as the Cosmos is part of co-creating each human, gently evolving shifts lie at the core of humanity and happen in waves. Thus, a few times in my life, I have watched as a new wave of consciousness arrives all wrapped up as a newborn baby. As these children grow, they introduce the rest of us to the evolutionary shifts in consciousness that are unfolding so that each of us can adapt more easily. Hence, around the year 2000, opalescent and luminous soul colours started showing up, including my daughter's.

Babies inspire joy and love in people around them. And not just human babies, but babies of all species. They can inspire radiance in your energy systems, activating your soul energy and your heart energy. These opalescent children take it to a whole different level.

Several times, I have been in rooms full of people and suddenly become aware of a movement, a field moving through the room that was impacting everyone. It was a field of joy. Energy field after energy field shifted and lit up, templates of health became activated, and a kindness switch was flipped on. The energy fields (the people) moved from habitual to creative, their flow expanded, and healing began. And all because someone with an opalescent soul colour had walked into the room. It is quite phenomenal.

Having observed this happen for over 19 years now, I have noticed it begins as soon as the young person walks into the room, whether or not they have been seen or noticed. As their energy fields inform the energy fields of the people closest to them, expansion begins and then spreads in waves throughout the room. And it is at no cost to the energy fields of the person with the opalescent soul colour; they remain contained, intact, coherent, and themselves. It is their soul joy, their soul kindness, that is expressed through their energy and informs the energy fields, and therefore the consciousness, of everyone in the room. How long this joy radiates through the energy fields of each person in the room depends on how much they are in relationship with their creative energy field rather than their habitual one, especially regarding how much stress they are experiencing.

Have you ever watched one of your favourite comedians and not laughed at all, yet another time, another day, you watched the same skit and roared with laughter? You know what you are in the mood for and whether you are able to find something funny or not. The skit stays the same, so it must be *you* that is different; your sense of humour just wasn't accessible that one day. What is the difference in

you from that day to the other? Stress, and the way it activates your habitual reactive field and moves you into fight–flight–freeze protection.

Your soul joy and soul compassion are always present for you. They never go; they never waver; they will always be informing your template of health and radiating through your body system. But there are times when this core joy isn't being picked up by the energy systems that usually carry it so thoroughly through your whole body system, for they are saturated in stress instead. Being in your fullness involves being able to dive beneath that fight–flight–freeze response and its corresponding chemicals and hormones, for under it, there is always joy. Sometimes, despite the stress, watching that comedian activates your joy that then explodes through your systems, dissolving the stress, healing the places in your body that stress had started to impact, and reactivating your kindness switch. Other times, those energy systems are a bit locked into the stress and you simply know you are not in the mood.

Several years ago, I remember reading a quote by the Dalai Lama that said, 'Be kind whenever possible.'[1] I took a quick assessment of myself and noted that, yep, I am a kind person. I am kind in many ways every day, and I choose kindness whenever I can. Great, checkmark. And then I read the next part of the quote: 'It is always possible.'

_____

[1] "His Holiness the Dalai Lama Spends the Day on Capitol Hill," DalaiLama.com, March 7, 2014, https://www.dalailama.com/news/2014/his-holiness-the-dalai-lama-spends-the-day-on-capitol-hill.

What? Really? *Always* possible to be kind? I felt a squirminess somewhere deep in my solar plexus. There are definitely times when I am not kind. Times when I snap at someone, lose my patience, or judge something about myself or another person. Sometimes I choose to let my husband get out of bed and put the cat out when I could extend kindness and let him stay warm and cosy! There are so many times, every day, when I could be kinder.

For many years, I have sat with the Dalai Lama's words, letting them play over and over through my awareness, my consciousness, and my entire energy system, and inviting their resonance to sink deeper and deeper. I have invited them to penetrate the places in my habitual field where I may be busy playing out a programmed way of being and forgotten that I have a choice, in every moment, no matter what is unfolding around or within me. I have welcomed the awareness that kindness is 'always possible' to radiate continually through my creative energy fields so that it becomes not only an active daily choice, but a state of being. 'Be kind whenever possible. It is always possible.' Wow.

Every day, I witness acts of kindness: the genuine smile of someone as they walk past me on the pavement, my husband bringing me a cup of tea unasked, a car stopping to let a pedestrian cross the road, someone holding the door of a shop open for another person . . . the list could go on and on. And I know that every day, you are part of that essential fabric of kindness. Thank you for every kindness you share and every kindness you receive, for every act of intentional kindness is massive and carries within it the potential to change the world.

I also witness daily acts of unkindness, oftentimes bordering on acts of cruelty. Do I live in such a horrible place that I see these constantly? No, but I see what happens in a person's energy fields when they think something unkind about themselves or judge themselves harshly. At best, this is unkind; at worst, it is cruel.

You might have been thinking that this chapter was going to be about being kind to other people. Of course that is essential, too, but unless you have embraced being kind to yourself, you will never be able to truly be kind to another person. Being kind to yourself is the biggest and most vital part of living your life to the fullest and is the foundation of all the other kindnesses you engage in.

I realise there might be aspects of this that you feel resistant about. Maybe you are thinking, 'Hey, wait a minute, Prune. I might think I look horrible every time I look in the mirror, but I can still be kind to other people.' Yes. And no. Or rather, yes, you can still be kind, but the vibration of kindness that you hold in you will be far less than when you have connected it all the way through *your* body system by always being kind to yourself.

When you are kind to others without first being kind to yourself, the place where your energy of kindness collapses is your solar plexus. Remember the description I gave at the beginning of this chapter of the energy of kindness? Well, the solar plexus chakra, or third chakra, lies between the root (first) chakra, sacral (second) chakra, and heart (fourth) chakra. When an explosion of kindness begins to activate through your whole body system, it hits a huge block in your third chakra and dissipates as if it has been sucked into a black hole, a vortex

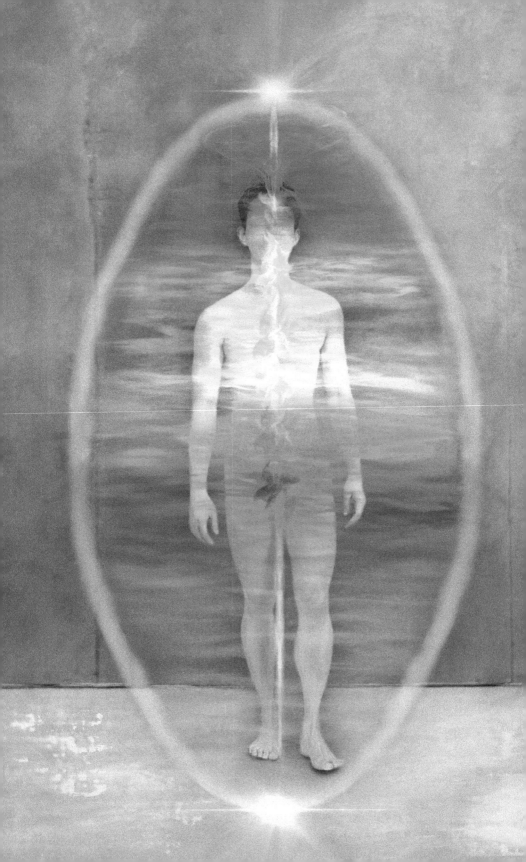

of self-criticism and self-judgement. This leaves your heart to be the only energy that can still engage in the expression of kindness as a soul joy, for your heart is connected directly into your energetic core and can bypass all the other systems that are depleted by the 'black hole' in your solar plexus chakra.

Now, it is *very* important to say that kindness from the heart is still beautiful and life-affirming. Every kind act you have ever engaged in has sent the vibrations of kindness, joy, and love into the web of life. That is powerful and essential healing, yet it is quite different from the profound and transformative potential of your entire system.

For a moment, let's stay thinking about that web of life. Let's say that for every act of kindness you engage in, you send a ripple of healing, loving, and conscious energy through the threads of the web. The vibration in those threads affects all of life. Now, let's say that for every unkind thought or act you engage against yourself, you non-consciously spread a ripple of unpleasantness through the threads of the web. This, too, affects all of life. What would your ratio of kind thoughts and actions versus unkind thoughts and actions be? What overall vibration are you sending out through those threads that is affecting all of life, including yours, mine, and the collective's?

A few years ago, I attended a shamanic retreat and was in the process of saying goodbye to my friends and colleagues as the retreat was ending. As I hugged one friend, James, he said

←———————

When you are kind to others without first being kind to yourself, the place where your energy of kindness collapses is your solar plexus.

to me, 'Thank you for all that you are doing, bringing so many gifts out into the world.'

'Thanks, James,' I replied. 'I appreciate that, though with all that is going on in our world, it never feels like it's enough.'

'How cruel,' he replied, as he squeezed my hand before turning to the next goodbye.

James had no idea how those words changed my life. My brain leapt to understand and track the truth in what he had just said. Cruel to be wanting to help the world? No. Cruel to be working so hard? No; maybe a bit tiring at times, but not cruel. Cruel to be feeling that my work was never enough? Hmm . . . That my amazing, beautiful, blessed work was never enough and therefore what I was doing was never enough? Hmm . . . Yes, that was harsh. Harsh to myself, and yes, cruel.

Though I understood and completely agreed, I had simply never seen it that way before. My dedication and determination to my work and my need to be making a difference had got in the way of understanding that even without any work, even without any of the determination, drive, and commitment, it was enough. *I* was enough.

From that moment on, I committed to consciously appreciating all that I created, all that I did, and even all that I didn't do. Perhaps I wasn't very effective at designing a course or writing a blog one afternoon, but instead of judging myself, I asked what I needed to nourish myself so that whatever was restless or tired within me could be nurtured instead. I came into a relationship of kindness and joy with myself. I blossomed, and with that, my work blossomed, too.

So many programmes in your habitual, reactive energy field play out and repeat the small (or big) unkindnesses that have somehow snuck in over the years of your life. And yet, now they are there, repeating the same words and blocking your soul joy from spreading through every part of your life.

- How are you unkind to yourself? Where might there be thoughts and acts of non-intentional cruelty happening in your daily life?

- Do you spend your time working or helping other people, only to collapse into a chair when you get home, eat a ready-made meal, and drop into bed, exhausted?

- Do you feel love for your body when you stand in front of your mirror naked, or do unkind thoughts come to mind?

- Do you get enough rest, sleep, and playtime to nurture yourself, or do you scramble from one 'must-do' in your busy life to the next, without being kind to your own body and your own needs?

- Do you chastise yourself when you make a mistake, perhaps telling yourself, 'I'm so stupid, how could I have done that? Another mess up, again!'?

- Are you in a relationship in which your partner doesn't support or respect your needs? If so, what words do you tell yourself to justify your partner's behaviour? That you should have done better? That you should have tried harder?

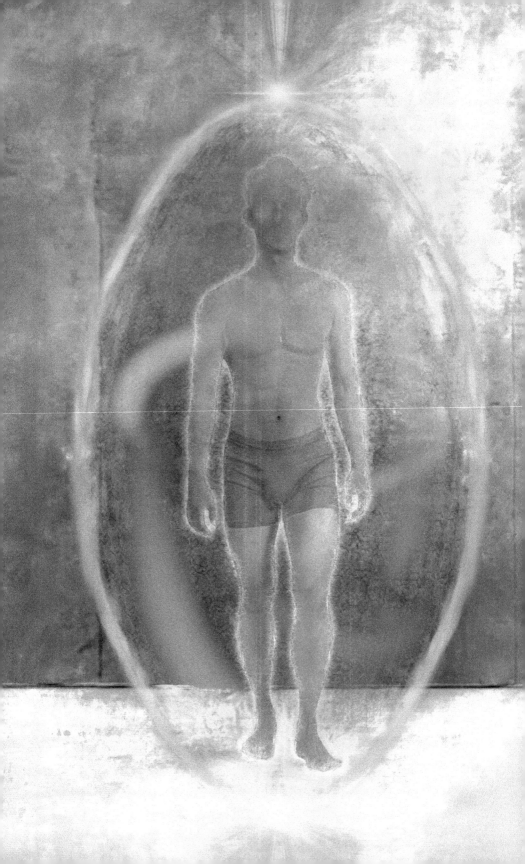

To experience the magnificence of living in kindness to yourself and therefore others, your energy system needs to be operating within your creative, responsive field. Remember that this brings awareness and the ability for conscious choice. It brings the awareness that your energy is the energy that creates the fabric of the universe.

ACTIVATING KINDNESS

Always treat yourself as if you are your best friend. For example, imagine if your best friend came home from work tired, stressed, and hungry; walked into the kitchen, which was a mess, because her teenagers had come home earlier and fed themselves; went to the fridge and found there was very little in it (because the teenagers had eaten it all); and then sat down and burst into tears. Would you tell her to get a grip, just deal with it, this is what life is like and next time do a better job of shopping so there is more to eat? Would you ask her why, since everyone else manages to work, cook, and shop, she can't do better? No, you wouldn't! You would likely make her a cup of tea, give her a tissue, say that you totally understand this is overwhelming, and tell her you are so sorry she had such a crappy day at work. Perhaps you would even pop down to the shop to pick up a few things for her to eat. Or maybe, if you are the assertive kind, you would call up to the teenagers and send

←————————————

Every act of kindness you engage in sends ripples of healing, loving, and conscious energy through the threads of the web of life.

them down to the shop instead while you have a cuppa with your friend. But you get my point.

Or try this one. Your friend tries on a dress in the changing rooms of a high-street clothing shop. Do you say, 'Oh my god, you look hideous in that dress. Look at your hips bulging out there, that is disgusting. And you are way too old for it, anyway. Look at the wrinkles on your chest, yuck, you have old-lady skin everywhere. You should have taken better care of yourself. You couldn't even lose weight on all of those diets. You are gross.'

Did I say cruel?

You would never say anything like that to your best friend! You would never even think anything like that about your best friend. And yet, have you said any of that to yourself? Maybe, at times, you have said all of it – or similar kinds of cruel, judgemental, criticism of yourself – about things other than your body. Maybe your unkind words centred around the value of your work ('He is much better at X than me'), your lovability ('I'm so Y, I won't ever have a successful relationship'), or your own physical beauty ('My nose is too big, my legs are puny, my jaw is too weak . . . ').

Your relationship with yourself is the foundation for every other relationship in your life. Can you be part of the revolution of not judging yourself? Once you are grounded into the depth of the compassionate kindness that runs through your own system, you can be truly, madly, and deeply kind. You resonate with it; it is just who you are. Just in case you are thinking it, that doesn't mean being a pushover or a sucker who is kind to everyone only to feel burnt out, exhausted, and taken for granted.

When you are connected into kindness towards yourself, it means you can easily set resilient boundaries. You know your generosity to others flows from your generosity to yourself, and that includes saying 'no' to requests you can't meet and 'yes' to resting when you are beginning to feel tired, even if someone else wants your help with something. Kindness to yourself means *sustainable* kindness, and everyone benefits.

Connecting into your kindness also means you are able to accept kindness from others. It often seems far more 'normal' at the moment for people to shun kindness or deflect it. It can be that you don't feel you deserve it, or it could be that you simply haven't yet practised receiving it because you spend so much time denying it to yourself in your own words or actions. But it is your soul's right for people to share deep kindnesses, big kindnesses, with you. So intend to receive them, and identify kindness wherever it presents itself. It is the most magnificent anchor for your whole life. Embrace it, share it, and wrap yourself up in it. You will be amazed at how much kindness there is in your life once you look for it and welcome it in.

Amy came to my clinic to get some support during her journey with breast cancer. By the time I saw her, she had had a double mastectomy and undergone chemotherapy. Her hair was gone, she was very thin, and she was terrified that her cancer would come back stronger next time. Her aura was like a lightbulb flashing on and off as it shifted between exhaustion and defence. Her fear impeded her heartfield, as well as the organ itself, with heart beats that clustered quickly and then slowed erratically. Her heart and her aura were telling the same story. Grounding was impossible, and with the kind of electrical disarray she was presenting with, no wonder she felt such fear and unsafety. Her system looked like one of the old TV screens that had black and white specks all over them, flashing on and off.

I had worked with plenty of people who had cancer, and many of them had chosen chemotherapy or radiation therapy, but I had never seen an energy field be quite so unable to restore itself as Amy's. What was going on?

A few sentences into her story and it started becoming clear.

'I never should have taken that job,' she said. 'I knew it was going to kill me. It was so bloody stressful; I knew it was going to kill me. It is entirely my fault that I got cancer. I knew it would break me.'

'And the way I used to eat and drink and party and smoke, and more, too. I've done this to myself, and now all my family is suffering because they are so worried about me.'

'I'm so stupid. I knew it, and I'm sure it's going to come back now. I can feel it still in my system.'

She was so scared and so desperate, all the kindness towards herself had hidden deeper and deeper inside as the pathways it would have travelled became filled with self-loathing and fear. The barrage of words against herself, her choices, and her actions was a barrage of energy against her body, her health, and her wholeness. Each time the spark in her system – the life force in her body – lit in activation, the energy of self-loathing would halt it. I can see it and feel it now as I write these words, and my heart constricts with compassion remembering it.

So I talked to Amy about the beauty of her unique soul colour, which was a rich amethyst vibration. I talked about the challenges of that particular colour (self-acceptance and self-love) and also the immense gifts that it offered (wisdom, connection between the head and heart, clarity of mind, and creativity, passion). She said it was as if I was describing how she was as a child. I kept talking, and she started crying.

Through her tears, Amy's memories of how she 'really is' flooded back to her: the laughter, the joy at being in nature, the hours of watching butterflies and listening to birds, reading stories under the covers with a flashlight long after her bedtime, the enjoyment of eating food at her kitchen table, flowers on the table. And as she remembered, it was as if her system took a massive (cosmic) sigh of relief and kicked back into action. The flashing on and off stopped and the glow of her life force began to move. It was slow and weak, but I could see it and her soul colour driving it forward. The lesson had been learned, the challenge overcome. The dark night of her soul was over.

After several sessions and over several months, it was as if the tangle of Amy's energy systems found their true pathways one by one. And at the foundation of each of the pathways was compassion for herself, kindness towards her body, and lots and lots of laughter.

THE BALANCE OF KINDNESS

Most of us know that the world is not (yet) harmonious and balanced. There are pains, confusions, and injustices everywhere you choose to look. And yet the power of kindness and compassion infuses every situation with the consciousness of potential, and this provides a bridge between, well, everything.

Kindness and compassion move everyone involved beyond narrow viewpoints of self-interest, self-protection, and polarisation towards the potential and wisdom of compassionate connection (from the habitual energy field into the creative energy field). It is from this place that creative solutions arise and the current mountain of problems can be dissolved. Knowing that kindness holds vast power, grand wisdom, and massive potential, can you commit to being kind to yourself? I think you can.

The energy of kindness, and its formative relationship with compassion and gratitude, invoke in your awareness the calling of the soul, for the more beautiful world you know is waiting for you and for all of the children of today and tomorrow. Kindness lifts the veil on some of the illusions and insecurities of modern life as the longing of your soul radiates from the back of your heart and connects with the soul of others, creating a different world for all to experience. And not just on the physical dimension; the energy of kindness moves through your ancestral field, healing those long dead in your family tree and clearing the way for those who are yet to come.

PRACTICES

 Thinking:
Celebrating Kindness

Think about and write down the answers to the following questions:

- What is the biggest kindness you have ever received?

- What is the biggest kindness you have given someone you love?

- What is the biggest kindness you have given a stranger?

- How can you be more kind today?

 Feeling:
One Minute, One World

This practice invites you to fully experience the flow of gratitude and involves breathing a full, nourishing breath in and out nine times, which will take about one minute. It can be deeply transformative for your own life as well as for all of us, as you are working on the personal level, the connective level, and the cosmic level. I hope you enjoy it.

1. Firstly, bring something or someone to mind that you are grateful for.

2. To experience your gratitude, tune into it and take three breaths while you think about that thing or person. You might want to follow this guide:

   a. I am grateful for (person, place, animal, object, institution, system).

   b. I am grateful because X.

   c. I welcome the energy of gratitude as it nourishes and nurtures every part of me.

   d. I breathe in gratitude and embrace it.

3. To share your gratitude, consciously choose to do so. Remember that your energy follows your thoughts, so simply by making this choice, your energy fields will respond. You might want to follow this guide:

   a. I share my gratitude with (person, place, animal, object, institution, system).

   b. I share my gratitude because X.

   c. Thank you for being part of my life.

   d. Thank you for being part of my world.

   e. I am so grateful for you.

4. To emanate gratitude into the web of life, take three conscious and expansive breaths. While doing so, choose to share your gratitude throughout the Cosmos and be an active part of co-creating a Cosmos where gratitude and kindness are part of every thread. You might want to follow this guide:

a. I am so grateful for all (people, places, animals, objects, institutions, systems).

b. I am so grateful for all who X.

c. I share my gratitude with all beings in this great collective web of life, including myself.

d. Thank you. (You can repeat this as many times as you wish.)

 Doing:

Talking the Talk

1. Stand in front of the mirror and look at yourself. You can be clothed or naked.

2. Start talking to yourself, expressing kindness. If this is totally alien to you and you don't even know where to start, start small. Choose to focus on a part of your body you are comfortable with and say, 'I like you' or 'I really like you,' or, if you are able, 'I love you.'

3. Choose another part of your body and begin to talk kindly to it.

4. If you are struggling, remember to think about what you would say to your best friend if this were their nose, thighs, abs, legs, hairy chin, or bald spot.

5. Your entire body will begin to change at the molecular level as the energy of kindness begins to move from, through, and around your body fields.

6. Choose to actively be more kind in how you talk to and think about yourself.

7. Make a commitment to being more kind to yourself, every day.

Remember, I have created videos of many of the practices in this book, so I can guide you as we do them together. You can find these videos and other supporting material at www.pruneharris.com/radiant-soul.

*Kind words can be short
and easy to speak, but their
echoes are truly endless.*

~Mother Teresa
(1910–1997)

15

YOUR WILD
WISDOM

The intuitive mind is a sacred gift and the rational mind is a faithful servant.

~Albert Einstein

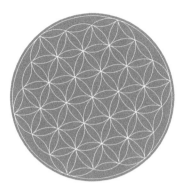

When was the last time you were struck by your awesomeness, your own ability, or your own wisdom? The last time you thought, 'Hey, that's right! I've never thought of it like that' or, 'OH! I understand!' or, 'YES! I am a GENIUS!'? I want this to happen to you every day. Because every time you experience a thought like this, it means you have welcomed a burst of your Wild Wisdom.

Your Wild Wisdom lives in every cell, every energy system, every part of your being. You may call it your intuition, imagination, perception, or emotional intelligence, or you may not call it anything at all. I call it your Wild Wisdom because it is so much bigger than any of that or any other boxed-in package.

Your Wild Wisdom is vast, magnificent, untamed, magical, and astute. It sees straight through deceptions, spins, and weasel words. It laughs at pronouncements, howls at dogma, and shudders at dumbed-down explanations of 'how things really are.' It stalks you as you plod methodically through your day, lost somewhere within the functioning of your habitual energy field. It rages every time you say, 'It is what it is' with a defeated resignation you call acceptance. It calls, prods, prompts, and reminds you as it walks alongside your every thought and your every emotion, inviting you to take one tiny step through its gateway.

And then it roars a different song through your dreams, your creative projects, your walks in the rain, and your times of passion and rage. It throbs a song of power, connection, peace, joy, and sensuality – a song of claiming the sheer lusciousness of life. It clamours for your attention, waiting to show you how to be all that it already knows you are, in all of your vast potential. You are hardwired for Wild Wisdom at every point of your energy. It never weakens; it never disappears; it never gives up on you. There is no escaping it, ever. Which means you have two choices: either you spend a huge amount of energy and effort avoiding or ignoring it, squishing it down, explaining your actions to it, and feeling less, or you throw open your arms, welcome it in, and embark on the greatest friendship of your life.

Creativity is not an add-on to daily life; creativity *is* life, and your Wild Wisdom knows this. I am not necessarily talking about the creativity of painting, writing, or singing, although those are all beautiful forms of creativity. I am referring to creativity as the awareness that your energy creates the fabric of the universe and that every moment of your existence adds to the creative process that Earth is continually involved in. This beautiful planet that is our home is not complete; it isn't 'finished.' It is evolving just as you are, just as we all are – every individual, every family, every community, every species.

Creativity is life, and life is creativity. And if you are reading this, then you are alive, which means you are already part of the creativity process, part of that web of life. This is true even if where you are in your life right now means you are living close to one percent on your scale of power, mostly from your habitual field. Even then, you are still alive, and your energy and body are still the repository of all of your genetic inheritance and all of your cosmic inheritance. Your body is continually involved in the creative process of growing cells, informing cells, recycling cells, falling apart, healing, and changing. With the life cycle of each cell, creativity brings you further into being, even if you don't bring your consciousness to it.

But what about if you do? What if you choose to commit to your soul expression in all its beauty and magnificence? What if you choose to engage consciously and actively in being part of your creative life force, your creative responsive energy field? Well, then, get ready for you and your Wild Wisdom to become best friends and have the ride of your lives together, quite literally! When you choose to commit to your soul and all of its unique and exquisite expression, you blossom and unfold; you come out of the cocoon and fly. You become you, and in doing so, you make it even more possible for everybody else to fully become, too.

SO WHY AREN'T YOU ALREADY DOING IT?

For several hundred years now, rationality has kind of ruled the show. Rationality is like a monarch sitting atop a hierarchical pyramid made up of the scientific process, reductionism, reason, and logical conclusions. In and of themselves, none of these things are a problem; they are all awesome when they are a *part* of the foundation of human society. But since the 1600s, they increasingly became elevated in their position of value and authority until political, financial, judicial, and many other systems placed their value well above holism, interconnectivity, and the understanding that, as human beings who are each a part of an immense living ecosystem, we have as many responsibilities as we have rights. Such systems relegated these understandings in favour of 'traditional knowledge,' overlooking the fact that it is the very nature of interconnectiveness that grounds human beings, communities, societies, and life itself in the continual process of becoming.

Not that Wild Wisdom can ever be erased from the human experience; it is far too, well, wild and wise for that! Wild Wisdom and love walk hand in hand, and therefore exist everywhere. But in this most recent phase of societal evolution (the last 400 years), it has become increasingly normal – perhaps even a requirement – to leave love at home. We are expected to show up in the workplace as a meagre persona of ourselves, replete with logic, rationalism, and ordered structure. Feelings at work? Emotions at work? Intuition at work? Ridiculous!

And yet, Wild Wisdom is rebellious and will always find a way: the detective who solves the case because of a 'gut feeling,' the doctor who discovers a cure because of a 'hunch' that turns out to be true, the woman who knows she is pregnant because of a dream, the stock broker who gets an intuitive hit that now is the time to buy or sell . . . the list can go on and on.

We even have a scientific explanation for the way in which our left brain (rational) and right brain (creative) embrace both the rational and creative aspects of ourselves and our life experiences. What we don't have an explanation for is why, even when our brains hold the qualities of rationality and creativity in equality, our societies don't. And let's be clear here. There has been amazing creativity, imagination, and deep wisdom occurring over the last few centuries, but the general societal narrative is based on the logical assumption that linear progress would provide the solution to all human challenges and ambitions. Now, we know that isn't true; our societal challenges are vast and increasing, and from this place of uncertainty, we get creative and ask many questions.

As with all times of unbalance and dilemma, it doesn't take Einstein to help us understand that we can't solve a problem at the same level of consciousness from which it was created. We need an energetic expansion, a shift in consciousness, and that is what every country in the world is currently going through. After hundreds of years spent gradually moving further away from soul connection, emotional balance, and physical health, billions of people are now questioning what is needed.

THE QUESTION IS USUALLY MORE IMPORTANT THAN THE ANSWER

So what *is* the answer? How do we solve the problems of the world? Don't worry about that. It isn't only ours to know. Throw away that level of responsibility, for it is crippling, disempowering, and overwhelming.

Answers to collective problems are found in the Wild Wisdom of the collective energy field, the collective consciousness. When enough people – including you – put their attention, their energy, and their consciousness there, the solutions will start evolving and can be transmitted through the human realm and into human reality. It is already occurring. You can engage in co-creating the questions, the answers, and the living solution, but that is not yours to do alone.

And what about your own life? What questions are waiting to be asked? Every time you create a question, your Wild Wisdom can provide answers. It is an answer beyond logic, beyond rationality. It is an answer nourished by the energy in the cosmic web of life, and because of this, it holds the consciousness of not only every life on Earth, but Earth itself, as well as the Sun, the Moon, and the stars.

Sometimes the hardest part in the entire process of transformation is knowing what questions to ask. Watching energy over the years, I have noticed that the most important questions to ask centre around the areas of your life where you feel the path is blocked or the door is closed.

Every time you create a question, your Wild Wisdom can provide answers.

If you know you have hit a plateau in your healing journey, then that is the place to ask the questions. If you see that all of your relationships seem to hold resentment, then that is a place to ask questions. If you just feel there is more to life than you are currently living, then that is the place to ask questions. And not the questions you have already been asking. They haven't worked. Your Wild Wisdom is inviting you to open the door of curiosity. It is waiting to help you ask the creative questions and, once you ask, will help you discover the answers as swiftly as possible.

Irritation, grumpiness, anger, weepiness, rage, resentment, despair, anxiety, and fear are all doors to deeper understandings. In every moment, you have the choice of ignoring and avoiding those closed doors, even though each one of them is taking a lot of effort to hold shut. Or, knowing your Wild Wisdom is just behind those doors, you can open them, get curious, and unveil the richness of treasures within.

In my clinical practice, I would often hear statements such as, 'I have been diagnosed with X [energetic full stop = door closed]' and, 'I had a miserable childhood [energetic full stop = door closed]' and, 'Since my divorce, I have felt incomplete [energetic full stop = door closed].' I want to encourage you to *never* have that full stop at the end of your sentence about yourself and *never* close the door on a statement, a feeling, or a way of being. Holding the space for your own possibility is the most powerful route to the deep healings that last a lifetime, and maybe beyond.

Imagine if 'I have been diagnosed with cancer [energetic full stop = door closed]' shapeshifts into 'I have cancer, and who knows what is next?' The door props open, even just a bit, and your Wild Wisdom readies itself to open it even more and show you how to heal. Or what if you shift to, 'I had a miserable childhood and I don't want my adult life to be like that'? The door opens, and Wild Wisdom whispers to you in every part of your life, pointing out beauty, illuminating kindnesses shown to you, and wrapping you up in love. And what if you shift to, 'Since my divorce, I have felt incomplete, and I'm bored sick of feeling like that. I want change.' Your energetic door becomes *wide open*, with Wild Wisdom dancing and singing, celebrating you.

No matter how you are feeling as you meet whatever is showing up in your life right now, erase the full stop in all of your defining stories and all of your definitive statements. Open the door to your own potential. The universe is looking to support you in all of your unique magnificence. Open the door and let it in, be curious, for Wild Wisdom is both born out of curiosity and the parent of it, too.

If you, like me, were raised in a society that warned 'curiosity killed the cat,' you can bring your creative curiosity to that statement and wonder why it needed to be so widely shared throughout society as a cautionary warning against being curious. Or you can listen to your Wild Wisdom as it reminds you that, throughout the world and across the ages, cats have been associated with magic, power, and transformation, and that there seems to be plenty of them still alive today. So curiosity can't be fatal, after all; in fact, it might just be magical!

Curiosity did not kill the cat; curiosity transformed lives.

Where can you shine your magical curiosity? What part of your life, your community, and our global challenges can be transformed by you getting curious, asking questions, and exploring your wild wisdom? What does the future need from you in order to become? Asking the questions opens the door, allowing the consciousness of potential to rush in. And from there, anything is possible, for you enter the imaginal realm.

THE IMAGINAL REALM

I love the imaginal realm. Truly. Like a dear beloved. I can't imagine my life without it, for I know it would be poorer, less colourful, and robbed of the daily magic that exists all around me.

Imaginal means 'relating to or pertaining to your imagination,' but hang on! I want you to understand what I mean by imagination. I use the word imagination in its original meaning, defined as 'direct perception through the inner eye of your heart.' Wow! So beautiful, isn't it? Imagination is not just something that you 'think' up, but belongs instead to the place of all potential that you access through your heart, your soul, and the collective empowerment of the imaginal realm.

The imaginal realm is a place of meeting. It is the energy field where your personal consciousness, the collective consciousness, and the supraconsciousness all meet and weave together, affecting, influencing, and co-creating every part of its whole (that means you!). You access the imaginal realm through your Wild Wisdom and your integrated heart, it meets it in your creative thinking and doing, your dreaming, your poetry, and your art, your humming, singing, and spontaneous dancing. It is the realm of your meditation and your contemplation, of your longing and of your mythic self. It is the realm of the possible, and you are not the only one in it.

⟶

Your aura has seven distinct vibrational layers, with the fifth housing your immense potential to connect into the richness of the imaginal realm.

As your aura expands from your skin to your auric membrane, it shifts through different vibrations to fully contain and connect all of your differing vibrational levels.

These could be perceived as different layers in the aura, and generally, I see seven distinct layers (although as with everything energetic, every layer has more layers if you care to explore them!). The fifth layer is the imaginal layer. If you were to extend your arm out now at the level of your chest and look at your forearm, the fifth layer will be level with the middle of your forearm. The imaginal layer holds the potential of who you are and how you are to do what you are here to do. It bridges the lower and higher vibration layers, and it activates every time your awareness moves towards or into the imaginal realm.

I am going to assume you have taken a photo using a smartphone and have used the filter settings that switch between the 'normal' representation of the photo and then all kinds of wonderfully named filters. Some make a photo sepia, some make it black and white, others change the ratio of light and dark in the picture to subtly give a different view, perspective, and lens to the image. When your imaginal layer activates, it is as if a filter has just turned up all the colours, blurred the edges a bit, and generally poured more light into the image.

Energetically, the imaginal realm is especially apparent in people who daydream, because they are very skilled at navigating consensual reality (or 'the real world'), even as they are also living in the imaginal realm. These people have a soft, shimmering energy running through their entire field, unless their attention is totally consumed with a daydream. In that case, the bright colours and dancing shimmer move in kaleidoscopic patterns.

Shamans have immense imaginal layers in their aura that are generally always active, as do psychics, mediums, people who channel, people who are in love, and children. People who co-create with nature, such as gardeners, sculptors, potters, and woodworkers, also have an imaginal layer that is continually active, as do those who work with nature spirits, such as herbalists, medicine women and men, and hedge witches. Some soul colours carry a naturally large imaginal layer, while others have a smaller one, but every single person has an imaginal layer. And when it is active, it not only informs all other vibrations in your body, but envelops, invites, embraces, and encompasses them, making each one a little fuller, a little more vibrant.

As I am writing this, I have a strong picture in my mind of the author and story wizard Neil Gaiman, for his is the biggest imaginal layer I have seen yet. The power of it even changes his electromagnetic field as he dives into the imaginal realm to meet the characters who will inhabit the stories pouring from his energy fields into his books.

The imaginal realm is a shared space, and you are never alone in it. The sentience of all living beings is held in a field of information and energy, and that means your energetic fields and fields of information form everything that has ever been, everything that is, and everything that ever will be and can be, all in communication. The imaginal realm is everything that has ever existed and can ever exist. It is a collective field of future, past, and present, where you are able to move outside the linear and logical constraints of time and space and leap into the possible, the potential, the quantum. From there, you understand, know, feel, perceive, sense, and absorb the vibrational wisdom that is all around and within you. And then you come back with both feet planted on the ground, your imaginal layer buzzing with information, and you change reality as you co-create the shift, the consciousness, the change you know to be possible. This can show up as a profound shift in your pathway of personal healing and evolution; a creative innovation that solves a personal, familial, or global challenge; or simply a beautiful reconnect with the fullness of yourself.

Your Wild Wisdom is the energy flying effortlessly between your imaginal realm and your energetic core, connecting your unique soul energy with the soul of the world and back again.

CONNECTING INTO THE IMAGINAL REALM

There are so many ways to enhance your energetic connection to your Wild Wisdom and imaginal realm. Firstly, know that you are already deeply connected to it through your dreams. Whether you remember your dreams or not, they will carry you in and out of the imaginal realm, for that is their place of birth and creation.

Here are my favourite ways to help people access their Wild Wisdom and create the easy bridges that allow them to travel back and forth, to and from the imaginal realm:

- Read fairy tales, myths, and legends from all over the world. Re-read them and then read them again. Every time you tap into the mythic, the mythic taps into you and activates the imaginal layer in your energy fields. This allows you to access the great archetypes of the human world, and it is through being in communication with these great archetypes that your consciousness rewrites your personal stories and myths.

- Listen to yourself. Talk to yourself. Ask yourself creative questions and then answer them. Remember, you are really talking with your best friend, your Wild Wisdom, but most other people won't know that!

- Open the doorway to the imaginal by closing your eyes, putting pen to paper, and writing whatever comes to mind. It may be prose, poetry, stream of consciousness, brilliance, or waffle. It will all be opening that doorway to the imaginal. Keep writing for 10 minutes, and never judge what you write.

- Intentionally give yourself time on your own – time to get curious, time to be lazy, time to daydream, time to hang out with your Wild Wisdom and get to know it more.

- Turn down the noise. It is difficult to hear your own wild wisdom when your head is full of other people's opinions of you, other people's insecurities,

other people's projections and perceptions. Take regular breaks from social media, and make a habit of having your TV off, rather than on. Each time you turn it on, make it a conscious choice, rather than something you do out of habit.

- Your energy is the bridge between the conscious, the subconscious, the supraconscious, and the daily. The more you understand your energy, the more you can nurture it and have the confidence to weave your life and our world into being.

- Ceremony exists in the imaginal realm and opens gateways between you and the Cosmos. In our modern-day societies, we are very used to the ceremonies of birthdays, weddings, and funerals, but every moment of every day is an invitation to engage in the ceremony of your life. Consciously lighting a candle and blessing your day is a ceremony. Sitting in the park and contemplating life and being an active part of the dreaming of the Cosmos is a ceremony. Joining with friends in collective meditation is a ceremony. So is honouring the passing of the year by celebrating the seasons, the equinoxes, and the solstices. There are so many ways you can bring the daily sacred into your life, and each way you do expands your imaginal energy field and nourishes you.

THE ENERGY OF WILD WISDOM

Your Wild Wisdom is always informing you as you engage in the continual flow of energy, information, and love between your own soul and the soul of the world. So many levels of energetic existence live within your human energy fields. Autonomic, habitual, and creative are simply levels within levels, fields within fields. You are never constrained by your energy, only by your understanding of and relationship with it. Remember that your energy fields are in a continual process of unfolding and enfolding, just as you are, and this means that no matter where you are right now, it is a phase in this perfect unfolding and enfolding. The next phase is already in motion.

In your whole energy field, there are no full stops, no straight lines, no fences of division. Every part of your energy field is connected to every other part of your energy field. It is not divisible, but instead forms dynamic, interconnective, pulsing, throbbing, thinking, feeling, living energy fields that make you *you*:

- Your energetic core taps you straight into the wisdom of the Cosmos.

- Your elemental rhythms gather the cosmic wisdom and unite it with the elemental wisdoms of Earth.

Your Wild Wisdom is always informing you as you engage in the continual flow of energy, information, and love between your own soul and the soul of the world.

- Your template of health carries these wisdoms as the consciousness of potential in every interface on the physical, emotional, and cosmic level.

- Your core wisdom radiates through all of your energy channels and all of your physical channels, flooding your blood with awareness.

- Each of your chakras carries its own vibration of your Wild Wisdom, feeding it to all else in your whole body system.

- Your aura conveys your Wild Wisdom into your daily life and the wisdom of your daily world back into your core.

- And at the centre of it all is your heartfield, housing and holding all of it like a magnificent cauldron filled with a magic potion, an imaginal potion. This potion is made from all of your creativity, all of your Wild Wisdom, all of your potential, and all of your consciousness.

Every time you choose to pay attention to yourself and your role as co-creator of the universe, that potion gets richer and richer, spreading through your body, your thoughts, your emotions, and your actions, and into every part of your life and the world beyond.

You have a unique and powerful purpose here, and it is to share this magic.

That is the energy of your Wild Wisdom.

That is the energy of you.

PRACTICES

 Thinking:
Meeting and Greeting Your Wild Wisdom

Think about what your Wild Wisdom would look like if it could appear before you as a human. Really allow your imagination to paint a vivid picture so that you can draw or describe exactly what this person looks like. This not only activates your connection to the imaginal realm, but brings you one step closer to meeting, greeting, and embracing your Wild Wisdom as your friend. Don't be surprised if this human picture you create starts showing up in your dreams and the times of your life when you need some help and guidance.

 Feeling:
The Love List

For this practice, you need a pen and paper, and make sure you have a lot of paper; no little scraps of paper for this list. You are going to write down all the things about yourself that are awesome and make you *you*. Now, don't get all squirmy on me about this practice. You are awesome, you are amazing, and I have spent an entire book explaining why. Now you need to believe it, too, and start your own list.

If you don't know where to start, here are some ideas:

- Think about what qualities you love in your friends and people you respect. It is highly likely (almost definite) that what you love and admire in other people is also part of your energy, which is why you are attracted to those qualities in others.

- Ask other people what they love about you and what they see as your best qualities.

- Don't settle for less than 100 points on your list. Yes, you are that amazing, and it is time to start recognising it, owning it, and hugging it close to you.

- Give yourself time. Perhaps you can easily write the first 25 points, but after that, it starts slowing down. Tuck it in your heart and mind and revisit it in a couple of days. You will find that your Wild Wisdom will have brought your attention to many more things by then.

- Be brave. Identifying your immense qualities isn't arrogant or selfish. It is knowing yourself, and that is one of the most important gifts you can give to both yourself and the world.

Doing:

Take those 100 points on your love list above and wrap them around you like a cloak of courage and soul song. Live your life in all of its beauty, in all of its authenticity. I love you, the world loves you; love yourself and be you. Do you. Every day, in every way.

Do not let your fire go out,
spark by irreplaceable spark in
the hopeless swamps of the
not-quite, the not-yet, and the
not-at-all. Do not let the hero
in your soul perish in lonely
frustration for the life you
deserved and have never been
able to reach. The world you
desire can be won. It exists,
it is possible, it is real, it is yours.

~Ayn Rand
(1905–1982)

16

'THE
IMAGINAL CELL,'
A BEDTIME STORY

Everyone knew it was impossible, until a fool who didn't know came along and did it.

~Albert Einstein

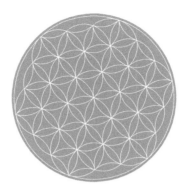

THE BUTTERFLY

There once was an egg attached to a leaf. Out of the egg came a caterpillar, who began to inch along the leaf. She was pretty happy. There was plenty of food around when she needed it (and she needed it A LOT!). She doubled her size in just a few days and just kept on eating. Some days, she got so big she had to grow a new skin to house her happy body in. She could eat and sleep, and all was OK within the great cycle of her daily life.

And then one day, she felt a bit funny. Like there was an itchiness inside her, a tickling buzziness that seemed to get more insistent with each passing day. It was like parts of her insides were kind of wiggly. A deep knowing (that she didn't even know she had until she was doing it!) made her create a little blanket home to rest in. She wove this home around

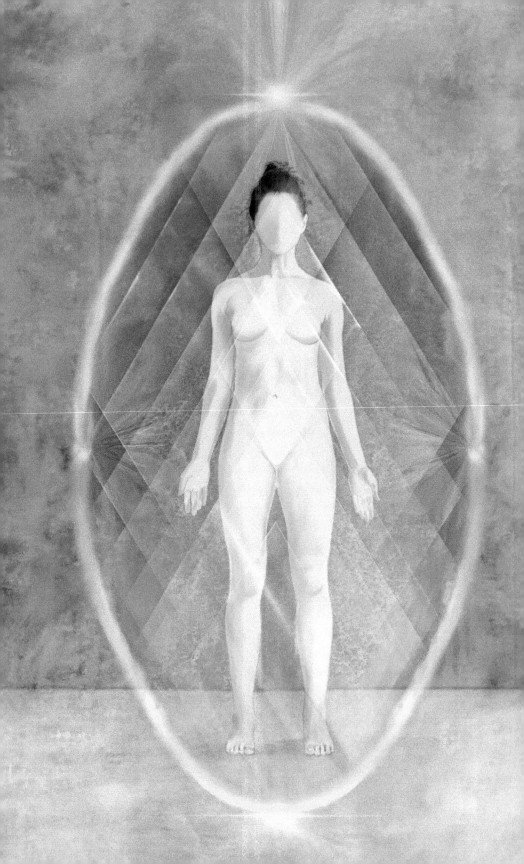

herself, and to anyone looking at her, it seemed that she got very, very still. She didn't move and just hung about. But inside that home, she was very, very busy. That funny buzziness inside her just kept rising, shifting something here, changing something there, pushing a little bit of skin here, and growing something extra there. She dozed, trusting and waiting as all that work was going on inside. Until one day, a deep knowing (that she didn't even know she had until she was doing it!) made her wiggle a bit, and gradually, her blanket home dropped away from her. She balanced on the leaf, warming her wings (wings?!), and then flew away as a colourful, vibrant butterfly.

Now, what this little caterpillar didn't know was that when she was born, she was born with all her regular cells that were functioning and working to just be her, *and* she also had other cells, called imaginal cells, that were doing nothing other than waiting. They were waiting for the right time. And when that time was right, when she was mature enough and ready enough, those cells were activated and began changing the function of the other cells. Gradually, they created a tiny cosmic soup from all the other cells, bringing forward a new awareness, a new way of being, a new field of consciousness to enable the transformation from caterpillar to butterfly.

THE BUTTERFLY IS YOU

There once was an egg growing inside a womb. Out of the womb came a baby, who began to inch through life. He was pretty happy. There was plenty of food around when he needed it (and he needed it A LOT!). He doubled his body size again and again and just kept on eating. One day, he got so big, he had to move out of his parent's home and begin to live his own life. He could eat and sleep and work, and all was OK within the great cycle of his daily life.

And then one day, he felt a bit funny. Like there was an itchiness inside him, a tickling buzziness that seemed to get more insistent with each passing day. It was like parts of his insides were kind of wiggly. A deep knowing (that he didn't even know he had until he was doing it!) made him take a good, long look at the society he was living in. He began to envisage a new home around himself, and to anyone looking at him, it seemed that he got very, very still (some people called this meditating). He didn't move and just hung about. But inside himself he was very, very busy. That funny buzziness inside him just kept rising, shifting something here, changing something there, pushing a little bit of awareness here, and inciting an extra conscious connection there. He dozed in his daily life, watching, waiting, and questioning as all that work was going on inside. Until one day, a deep knowing (that he didn't even know he had until he was doing it!) made him wiggle a bit, and gradually, his cocoon dropped away from him. He balanced on the edge of global consciousness, warming his body in the warm light of his own soul, and then opened his wings as a colourful, vibrant human, lighting the way for others to undergo their own transformation.

Right now in your life, you may be in the caterpillar stage, you may be in the internal buzziness phase, or you may be in the cocoon. You may be stretching your wings getting ready to fly, or you may already be flying around the world singing the song of your soul. Wherever you are in your personal life story, you are the imaginal cell, and each of us is waiting for you to activate.

THE BUTTERFLY IS US

There once was an egg growing inside the womb of the universe. Out of the universal womb came a blue and green planet that gradually came to be the home of a few humans. The humans began to inch through their lives and were pretty happy. There was plenty of food around when they needed it (and they needed it A LOT!). They doubled their numbers again and again and just kept on eating and growing. One day, they got so big, they had to grow a whole new way of being. The first time it happened, they called it the Agrarian Revolution, and the second time it happened, they called it the Industrial Revolution. The humans could eat and sleep and work, and eat and sleep and work, and eat and sleep and work, and work and work and work and work. They hit the alcohol and drugs hard, they hit the television hard, they hit work harder, and they hit each other, and all was not quite OK within the great cycle of their daily lives.

And then one day (to no surprise), they began feeling a bit funny. Like there was an itchiness inside them, a tickling buzziness that seemed to get more insistent with each passing day. It was like parts of their insides were kind of wiggly, not quite happy, not quite content, and not quite willing to put up with what had been created. A deep knowing (that they didn't even know they had until they were doing it!) made them have a good, long look at the society they were living in. They began to envisage a new home around themselves, and to anyone looking at them, it seemed that they got very, very still, pensive, and a bit grouchy. They didn't move and just hung about. But inside they were very, very busy. That funny buzziness inside them just kept rising, shifting something here, changing something there, pushing a little bit of awareness here, and inciting an extra conscious connection there. They observed their daily lives, watching, waiting, and questioning, as all that work was going on inside. They shed their layers of isolation, their layers of insecurity, their layers of unexamined assumptions, and their layers of sleepy acceptance, until one day, a deep knowing (that they didn't even know they had until they were doing it!) made them wiggle a bit and reach out and connect, and gradually, the cocoon dropped away from them. Together, they spread their wings, they were colossal and powerful, and they flew, creating a new global consciousness to nurture all of creation. Together, they created a new way of being for all imaginal souls from all walks of life and all forms of sentience, and together, they saved the soul of the world.

*I hope you will go out and let
stories, that is life, happen to
you, and that you will work with
these stories from your life – not
someone else's life – water them
with your blood and tears and
your laughter till they bloom,
till you yourself burst into bloom.
That is the work. The only work.*

~Clarissa Pinkola Estés
(1945–present)

Book Glossary

Ancestor

A person in your family who is no longer living. Your ancestors span from your direct parentage back to the very first humans who walked the Earth. Many cultures understand that animals and the natural world are also our ancestors.

Ancestral field

The energy field that contains all of the energetic information of your ancestors. You are part of this ancestral field and are influenced by it as well as being an influencer within it.

Archetypes

'Archetype' is a Greek word meaning 'original pattern.' They are universal symbolic patterns in our cultural myths, stories, and beliefs.

Assemblage Point

The assemblage point is part of your energy anatomy located 50 centimetres or so off the body in the vicinity of the upper chest. It acts as a magnificent energetic interface point between your daily and sacred life.

Aura

Your aura is a dynamic system of connective webbing that surrounds your physical body. It is created by the electrical and subtle energy fields of your body and is a connective, protective system which carries information through the rest of the energy system. Your aura conveys your Wild Wisdom into your daily life and the wisdom of your daily world back into your core.

Auric membrane

The auric membrane is the surrounding edge of your aura/biofield. The membrane is thick, and has an elastic quality so it can act as a buffer for your soul needs, letting through what is in service to your continued emergence and preventing other energy from entering your aura.

Biofield

An alternate term for your aura.

Energetic Core

Part of your energy anatomy, your energetic core is housed through the centre of your body. It holds your essential/soul energy, and brings in cosmic energy from above and below via your *Earth star* and *Sun star*.

Ceremony

A ceremony is the sacred container for a conscious and connective act of intention. This conscious and connective act of intention can often be performed physically through a ritual. One or more rituals can be part of a single ceremony, and usually is.

Chakras

Part of your energy anatomy, there are seven main chakras, each connected together through a central core. The word 'chakra' comes from the Sanskrit word meaning 'disc,' for each chakra moves in both a horizontal swirling motion like a disc, from your energetic core to the edge of your auric field.

Consciousness

Consciousness can be defined as 'awareness of your own internal states, as well as the events going on around you.' Energetically, consciousness means active engagement with the relational aspect of every part of your life.

Core Soul energy

The Core Soul energy is the deepest energy that runs within your energetic core and connects above and below.

Cosmic being

A sentient being such as a human, a tree, an animal, a guide. You!

Cosmos

The entire universe, considered as a unified whole; the great web of life.

Dantians

Dantian is a Chinese word meaning 'elixir of life,' and refers to three energy centres that reside within the energetic core. Individually, they are the lower, middle, and upper dantians.

Doshas

A dosha is a body type defined by the ancient Indians, who combined their intricate and complex elemental understandings of space, air, water, earth, and fire to identify three body types, or doshas, known as *kapha*, *pitta*, and *vata*.

Duality Consciousness

Also known as 'separation consciousness,' this is where you perceive yourself as separate and distinct from others, as opposed to 'unity consciousness,' which is where you are able to perceive your active role within the whole.

Earth Star

Positioned about a metre below your feet, the *Earth star* is a powerful energy centre that connects you with the Earth beneath your physical body.

Electrics system

Part of your energy anatomy, your electrics system manages the electromagnetic energy throughout your whole body system.

Elemental rhythms

Part of your energy anatomy, your *elemental rhythms* are vibrations that mirror the elemental energy of the Cosmos. You house these elemental energies from deep inside your energetic core and radiate them through all that you are.

Energy

Energy is the life-force of the Cosmos. It moves in patterns and waves and is encoded information.

Energy Channels

Part of your energy anatomy, these are pathways that send energy to specific parts of your whole body system. Your three main energy channels are the nadis, or songlines, the extraordinary channels, and the organ meridian system.

Energy fields

An energy field is an invisible force with an organising principle that is encoded with information.

Energy anatomy

The energetic structure that both creates and houses the energy systems of every living being.

Energy perception

The gathering of information, identification, and interpretation of sensory information about your energy in order to understand, integrate, and potentially act on the information.

Energetic cohesion

When your energy systems are balanced and working together.

Energetic core

Part of your energy anatomy, your energetic core is a super-highway of encoded light energy running through the centre of your body from above and below. Your energetic core houses your essential/soul energy.

Energetic sensitivity

Being able to feel, sense, or perceive the energy in and around you.

Energetic resilience

The ability to recover easily and quickly from external or internal energetic imbalance, such as extreme emotions, electromagnetic pollution, and stressful situations.

Energy systems

A system is a group of interrelated elements that form a unified whole. Energy systems work in exactly the same way, and there are six of them: the energetic core, the aura or biofield, the *elemental rhythms*, the energy channels, the chakras, and the heartfield.

Fascia

A thin layer of connective tissue that surrounds every individual part of your physical anatomy. For example, each of your muscles, organs, bones, nerve fibres, and blood vessels are wrapped in fascia.

Fields of consciousness

Everything about your energy fields serves you in your journey of becoming; they are your fields of consciousness and carry connectiveness at every level.

Figure 8s

(see Lemniscates)

Functional field

An energetic vibration, the functional field gives form and function to your energy systems. It provides support for the structure and processes of your energy anatomy.

Groundedness

Being grounded means that energy is flowing up from the Earth, through your feet, through your energetic pole, and out of your head, as well as in the opposite direction; from the crown of the head, through your energetic pole, and then through your feet, into the Earth. When you are grounded, you feel safe, solidly present, able to think clearly and process information well; you feel energised and stable. You feel nourished by the very ground that you are standing on.

Habitual field

An energetic vibration, the habitual field shows up in your energy systems when you are simply acting on habit. You aren't consciously engaging with your thoughts, emotions, or actions, you are just thinking, feeling, and doing them because that is what you do.

Heartfield

Part of your energy anatomy, your heartfield is created from the magical meeting point between your energetic core and the organ of your heart. It acts as a vast and conscious processing centre, absorbing energetic information from above, below, within, and outwith.

Hedge witches

A person who is experienced with deep study of, understanding of, and relationship with healing and magical energy of plants and the natural world. Often solitary practitioners, the hedge witch can also be known as a wise woman/man or medicine woman/man.

Human energy system

The human energy system is the energetic anatomy that forms a human (you!). It governs and determines your physical, emotional, cognitional, and spiritual functioning and experiencing throughout your life.

Imaginal

'Imaginal' means 'relating to your imagination.' Remember, we are not using the limited definition of imagination, meaning just your 'thinking' imagination, but the original definition of the word, which means 'direct perception through the inner eye of your heart.'

Imaginal Realm

The imaginal realm is a place of meeting. It is the energy field where your personal consciousness, the collective consciousness, and the supraconsciousness all meet and weave together, affecting, influencing, and co-creating every part of its whole (that means you!). You access the imaginal realm through your Wild Wisdom and your integrated heart; it meets it in your creative thinking and doing, your dreaming, your poetry, and your art, your humming, singing, and spontaneous dancing. It is the realm of your meditation and your contemplation, of your longing and of your mythic self. It is the realm of the possible, and you are not the only one in it.

Imaginal Cells

These are cells, present in caterpillars from the time of their conception, that hold the energetic information for the metamorphosis that is going to take place to turn the caterpillar into the butterfly. As the time approaches, the imaginal cells cluster together, acting together, and exchanging energy/ information by resonating at the same frequency. To someone who hears energy, they literally sing the new butterfly form into being! All of the other cells in the caterpillar dissolve in service to the emergence of this new form, the cocoon protects and nurtures this emergence, and the butterfly is born.

Imagination

I use the word 'imagination' and 'imaginal' through the original definition of the word, which means 'direct perception through the inner eye of your heart.' Wow! So beautiful, isn't it? Not just something that you 'think' up, but that you access through your heart, your soul, and the collective empowerment of the imaginal realm.

Ionosphere

The upper part of the Earth's atmosphere, where it meets space.

Kapha

In Ayurvedic medicine, kapha is one of the doshas, or body types.

Life force

The essential energy of creation. Other names are chi, ki, prana, spirit, vital force. It is the manifest energy of the entire universe and you are a part of it, for it moves in you, through you, around you, and from you.

Lemniscate

A lemniscate is a figure 8 shaped curve, sometimes known as the infinity symbol. It is a constant energy form, with your energy system holding billions of leminscates carrying information throughout your energy fields.

Magnetosphere

The Earth protects itself (and you) from the vastness of solar energy by having its own magnetic field, known as the magnetosphere.

Medium

Someone who serves as an intermediary between the living and the dead, empowering communication between the two.

Meridian

Part of your energy anatomy, meridians are channels that carry the flow of energy in directed pathways throughout your body.

Morphogenic field

This field is built through species-specific vibratory patterns, known as morphic resonance, which organise the bodies of plants and animals, and underlie their abilities to regenerate and heal. Morphogenic fields also coordinate the vibratory activities of the nervous system, and are closely connected to mental activity. It is this field that taps into and creates a collective consciousness. It is shared with the entire human race and is where cellular and soulular memory interacts and communicates.

Nadis

Part of your energy anatomy, your nadis are channels of energy. The word 'nadi' derives from the Sanskrit word 'nad,' meaning 'hollow stalk, sound vibration, and resonance,' for your 72,000 nadis are vibrating, resonating channels that create an interconnective web of energy through and around your entire body.

Nature spirits

The in-dwelling spirits that exist throughout the natural world.

Pitta

In Ayurvedic medicine, pitta is one of the doshas, or body types.

Plexus

An area in the body where a network of nerves, blood, or lymph vessels comes together.

Portal

An entranceway or point of connection to a deeper part of the body's energy systems.

Psychic

Someone who is able to access and interpret information in the collective and cosmic energy fields.

Radiant Soul energy

Your Radiant Soul energy flows from your Core Soul and radiates through all that you are.

Realm

A region or space. An organised energetic field that is contained.

Resilience

The capacity to recover quickly from difficulties. Energetic resilience is when your energy fields can hold or quickly resume their cohesiveness, and hold their creative field vibration rather than resort to the habitual field.

Shaman

The term 'shaman' comes from the Manchu-Tungus word 'šaman,' extended from the verb ša- 'to know;' a shaman is therefore literally 'one who knows.' Shamans are the weavers and walkers between the worlds, working to maintain balance in the web of life. In respect of the heritage of Indigenous shamans, and the desire not to engage in cultural appropriation, most of those trained shamanically in Western traditions choose to call themselves shamanic practitioners.

Soul energy

The energy in your whole body system that carries and expresses your soul. It is the brightest, lightest, highest vibration, and it shines through every other energy within and around that person.

Soul colour

Colour is a vibration. The vibration of your unique soul energy is known as your soul colour. Originating in your energetic core, it emanates through your radiant soul energy so that every cell is bathed in soul colour. Your skin is resonant with your soul colour, and as it continues through the energy field that surrounds your physical body, the soul colour spreads out to the very edge of your aura.

Stellar energy

A field of energy, and therefore information, that radiate from the stars and planets.

Stress repatterning points

Energetic portal points on your forehead which, when held or covered by your hand, can bring balance to your energy and help reprogramme your habitual, reactive, stress responses.

Subconscious

The part of your mind that you are not aware of, but which influences your actions, thoughts, and feelings.

Sun Star

Part of your energy anatomy, your *Sun star* is a powerful energy centre located a metre or so above your head. It is the top of your energetic core and is the interface point between your contained energy field and the cosmic energy fields above.

Taiji Pole

Part of your energy anatomy, the Taiji Pole is a component of your energetic core. Given this name by the ancient Chinese, it is an energetic pole that goes through the centre of your whole body system, and holds your vibrational essence/soul. Energy moves through it both ways continuously, and it looks like a super-highway of light filaments flowing through the very centre of you, connecting you to the Cosmos and the web of life.

Template of health

The energetic template that holds the coding of both your potential and your perfection. It is created at the magical meeting point where your energetic core meets the rest of your system and is repeated at every point of connectivity within your body.

The Soul of the World
The world soul is the sentient and loving universal consciousness that permeates the web of life, connecting all beings.

Unity Consciousness
A level of vibration/being/consciousness that goes beyond the concept of yourself as separate, and instead holds awareness of your interconnectivity with all of creation. It manifests as a sense of oneness, compassion, love, and respect, both for human beings, for nature, and for the universe.

Wild Wisdom
Your Wild Wisdom is your whole and connective way of knowing. It is the sum of your energy fields of consciousness, connecting your unique soul energy with the soul of the world and back again, calling you into more and more fullness and reminding you that you are always beloved and essential.

Yata
In Ayurvedic medicine, yata is one of the doshas, or body types.

Yin and yang
Originating from Chinese philosophy, yin and yang is a concept that describes opposite forces that are always in deep relationship. The existence of one is defined by the existence of the other.

Dear reader,

Thank you for reading this book and joining the Publish Your Purpose community! You are joining a special group of people who aim to make the world a better place.

What's Publish Your Purpose About?

Our mission is to elevate the voices often excluded from traditional publishing. We intentionally seek out authors and storytellers with diverse backgrounds, life experiences, and unique perspectives to publish books that will make an impact in the world.

Beyond our books, we are focused on tangible, action-based change. As a woman- and LGBTQ+-owned company, we are committed to reducing inequality, lowering levels of poverty, creating a healthier environment, building stronger communities, and creating high-quality jobs with dignity and purpose.

As a Certified B Corporation, we use business as a force for good. We join a community of mission-driven companies building a more equitable, inclusive, and sustainable global economy. B Corporations must meet high standards of transparency, social and environmental performance, and accountability as determined by the nonprofit B Lab. The certification process is rigorous and ongoing (with a recertification requirement every three years).

How Do We Do This?

We intentionally partner with socially and economically disadvantaged businesses that meet our sustainability goals. We embrace and encourage our authors and employee's differences in race, age, color, disability, ethnicity, family or marital status, gender identity or expression, language, national origin, physical and mental ability, political affiliation, religion, sexual orientation, socio-economic status, veteran status, and other characteristics that make them unique.

Community is at the heart of everything we do – from our writing and publishing programs to contributing to social enterprise nonprofits like reSET (https://www.resetco.org/) and our work in founding B Local Connecticut.

We are endlessly grateful to our authors, readers, and local community for being the driving force behind the equitable and sustainable world we are building together.

To connect with us online, or publish with us, visit us at www.publishyourpurpose.com.

Elevating Your Voice,

Jenn T Grace

Jenn T. Grace
Founder, Publish Your Purpose

About the Author

Prune Harris has grown up in a world of energy, and for the past 50 years, she has been tracking, understanding, and now translating this world for us all to experience. Since birth, Prune has been able to see energy: the energy of humans, animals, trees, and the Earth, showing up as vibrations and colours. Her simple and insightful explanations of how our personal energy field, our collective energy field, and the global energy field interconnect sheds forgotten light on how we can begin to move back to patterns of not just individual, but global health and harmony.

Through her in-person and online courses, Prune has empowered thousands of people across the globe to bring consciousness to their energy systems, because once we are aligned with our own template of health, we can then begin to align with the global template of health and, in her own words, 'That is where the real magic happens, for you, me, and our entire world.'

WE WOULD LOVE TO SUPPORT
YOUR RADIANT SOUL JOURNEY

Get the most out of this book with;

- Video Guides – Let Prune guide you through the practices in this book.

- 3 Months Free Membership – Join our online community at The Gathering Ground where you can share, connect, and be inspired.

- Do you want to know your soul colour? – As a gift, we would like to give you Prune's book '*What is the colour of your soul?*'

Visit www.pruneharris.com/radiant-soul or scan the QR code

NOTES

The B Corp Movement

Dear reader,

Thank you for reading this book and joining the Publish Your Purpose community! You are joining a special group of people who aim to make the world a better place.

What's Publish Your Purpose About?

Our mission is to elevate the voices often excluded from traditional publishing. We intentionally seek out authors and storytellers with diverse backgrounds, life experiences, and unique perspectives to publish books that will make an impact in the world.

Certified

Corporation

Beyond our books, we are focused on tangible, action-based change. As a woman- and LGBTQ+-owned company, we are committed to reducing inequality, lowering levels of poverty, creating a healthier environment, building stronger communities, and creating high-quality jobs with dignity and purpose.

As a Certified B Corporation, we use business as a force for good. We join a community of mission-driven companies building a more equitable, inclusive, and sustainable global economy. B Corporations must meet high standards of transparency, social and environmental performance, and accountability as determined by the nonprofit B Lab. The certification process is rigorous and ongoing (with a recertification requirement every three years).

How Do We Do This?

We intentionally partner with socially and economically disadvantaged businesses that meet our sustainability goals. We embrace and encourage our authors and employee's differences in race, age, color, disability, ethnicity, family or marital status, gender identity or expression, language, national origin, physical and mental ability, political affiliation, religion, sexual orientation, socio-economic status, veteran status, and other characteristics that make them unique.

Community is at the heart of everything we do—from our writing and publishing programs to contributing to social enterprise nonprofits like reSET (https://www.resetco.org/) and our work in founding B Local Connecticut.

We are endlessly grateful to our authors, readers, and local community for being the driving force behind the equitable and sustainable world we are building together.

To connect with us online, or publish with us,
visit us at www.publishyourpurpose.com.

Elevating Your Voice,

Jenn T Grace

Jenn T. Grace
Founder, Publish Your Purpose

Ingram Content Group UK Ltd.
Milton Keynes UK
UKHW020108100423
419832UK00012B/172